CORE SKILLS

GRADE

3

Math

ISBN-13: 978-0-7398-5725-0   **ISBN-10: 0-7398-5725-8**

2002 Edition, Harcourt Achieve Inc.
Copyright © by Harcourt, Inc.

Printed in the United States of America.

12 0982 11
4500299315

Steck-Vaughn™

A Harcourt Achieve Imprint

www.Steck-Vaughn.com
1-800-531-5015

Core Skills: Math
Grade 3
Table of Contents

Core Skills: Math, Grade 3, Table of Contents (cont.)

Core Skills: Math, Grade 3, Table of Contents (cont.)

Mental Math:
Fact Families

Write the set of numbers for each fact family.

1. 4 + 8 = 12; 8 + 4 = 12; 12 – 4 = 8; 12 – 8 = 4   _4 8 12_

2. 6 + 7 = 13; 7 + 6 = 13; 13 – 7 = 6; 13 – 6 = 7   _6 7 13_

Write the fact family for each set of numbers.

3. 7, 8, 15

$$7 + 8 = 15$$
$$8 + 7 = 15$$
$$15 - 8 = 7$$
$$15 - 7 = 8$$

4. 9, 4, 13

$$9 + 4 = 13$$
$$4 + 9 = 13$$
$$13 - 9 = 4$$
$$13 - 4 = 9$$

5. 6, 8, 14

$$6 + 8 = 14$$
$$8 + 6 = 14$$
$$14 - 8 = 6$$
$$14 - 6 = 8$$

Find the missing number to complete each fact.

6. 9 + _6_ = 15   6 + _9_ = 15   15 – _6_ = 9   15 – _9_ = 6

Mixed Applications

7. Ethan had 7 jungle animal stickers. He got 8 more. Write a number sentence to tell how many he has now.

   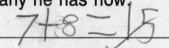 _7 + 8 = 15_

8. Write the three other facts in the same fact family.

   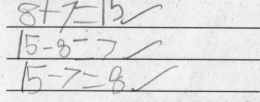
   _8 + 7 = 15_
   _15 – 8 = 7_
   _15 – 7 = 8_

VISUAL THINKING

9. What two facts describe this domino?

   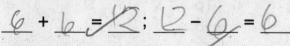 _6 + 6 = 12; 12 – 6 = 6_

   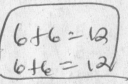
   _6 + 6 = 12_
   _6 + 6 = 12_
   _12 – 6 = 6_
   _12 – 6 = 6_

10. Why are there only two facts?

   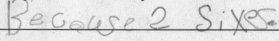 _Because 2 sixes_

9

Addition and Subtraction
Missing Addends

Find the missing addend.

1. $5 + 7 = 12$

2. $3 + 9 = 12$

3. $6 + 7 = 13$

4. $8 + 8 = 16$

5. $9 + 6 = 15$

6. $8 + 9 = 17$

7. $4 + 9 = 13$

8. $5 + 7 = 12$

9. $5 + 9 = 14$

10. $6 + 6 = 12$

11. $9 + 3 = 12$

12. $8 + 6 = 14$

13. $7 + 8 = 15$

14. $7 + 7 = 14$

15. $9 + 9 = 18$

16. $4 + 8 = 12$

17. $2 + 9 = 11$

18. $5 + 6 = 11$

Mixed Applications

19. Howard Husky, a race dog, runs 6 miles the first day of training. His total after two days is 11 miles. How many miles does Howard run the second day?

    $11 - 6 = 5$

20. Ms. Butcher has 8 dogs on her racing team when training season begins. By the end of the season, she has 15 dogs. How many dogs does she add to her team?

    $15 - 8 = 7$

MIXED REVIEW

Find the sum or difference.

1. $\begin{array}{r} 8 \\ +5 \\ \hline 13 \end{array}$

2. $\begin{array}{r} 5 \\ +9 \\ \hline 14 \end{array}$

3. $\begin{array}{r} 13 \\ -7 \\ \hline 6 \end{array}$

4. $\begin{array}{r} 16 \\ -8 \\ \hline 8 \end{array}$

5. $\begin{array}{r} 9 \\ -9 \\ \hline 0 \end{array}$

6. $\begin{array}{r} 7 \\ +7 \\ \hline 14 \end{array}$

7. $9 + 9 = 18$

8. $15 - 7 = 8$

9. $12 - 4 = 8$

Exploring Estimation
Rounding

Round to the nearest ten cents or the nearest ten.

1. 43 _40_
2. 79 _80_
3. 89 _90_
4. 61 _60_

5. 33¢ _30¢_
6. 47¢ _50¢_
7. 62¢ _60¢_
8. 85¢ _80¢_

9. 54 _50_
10. 58¢ _60¢_
11. 19 _20_
12. 45¢ _40¢_

Write the numbers in each row that round to the number in the box.

13. 85   83   78   75   73   88   [80]   _85 83 78_

14. 63¢   71¢   65¢   67¢   69¢   [70¢]   _69¢, 67 71¢_

15. Write the numbers that round to 10.
_9, 8, 7,_

16. Kathy estimates that she saw about 50 geese at the pond. What is the least number of geese she may have seen? the greatest number?

_40   60_

17. Kathy's suitcase weighs between 20 and 30 pounds, but she thinks it weighs closer to 20 pounds. What could the weight of her suitcase be?

_21_

CONSUMER CONNECTION

49¢   45¢   53¢   59¢   63¢

18. You are told that you can spend "about 50¢" at the toy store. Which items can you choose from?

a pen or a memo book

Estimation
Rounding to the Nearest Hundred

Use the number line. Round each number to the nearest hundred.

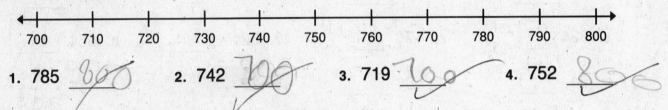

700 710 720 730 740 750 760 770 780 790 800

1. 785 _800_   2. 742 _700_   3. 719 _700_   4. 752 _800_

Round each number to the nearest hundred.

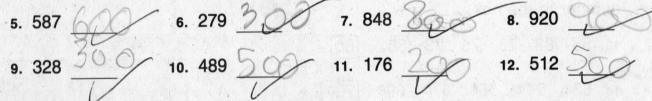

5. 587 _600_   6. 279 _300_   7. 848 _800_   8. 920 _900_

9. 328 _300_   10. 489 _500_   11. 176 _200_   12. 512 _500_

Write the number that is halfway between the two hundreds.

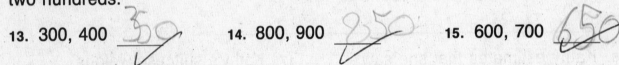

13. 300, 400 _350_   14. 800, 900 _850_   15. 600, 700 _650_

Mixed Applications

16. A jet crew is made up of 2 pilots, 8 flight attendants, and 1 flight supervisor. How many people are in the crew?

_11_

17. The small jet carried 378 people from New York to Washington. To the nearest hundred, about how many people were on the flight?

_400_

NUMBER SENSE

18. Does rounding to the nearest ten or rounding to the nearest hundred give a closer estimate? Explain.

Example
378
to the nearest ten—380
to the nearest hundred—400

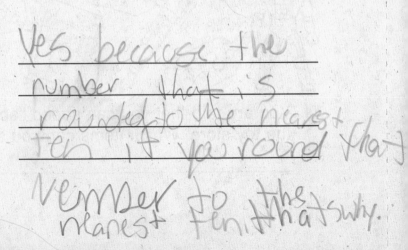

Yes because the number that is rounded to the nearest ten if you round that number to the nearest ten that's why.

Subtracting
Regroup Tens and Hundreds

Find the difference.

1. 546
  − 459
  _____
  187

2. 949
  − 368
  _____
  581

3. 815
  − 438
  _____
  377

4. 746
  − 209
  _____
  537

5. 912
  − 798
  _____
  114

6. 869
  − 679
  _____
  190

7. 452
  − 317
  _____
  135

8. 546
  − 281
  _____
  265

9. 515
  − 495
  _____
  20

10. 728
  − 384
  _____
  344

11. 219 − 68 = 151

    219
  − 68
  _____
  151

12. 489 − 392 = 77

    489
  − 392
  _____
  77

Mixed Applications

13. In June, Hank jogged 181 miles and Marcie jogged 214 miles. How many more miles did Marcie jog than Hank?

    214
  − 181
  _____
  33

  33 miles

14. Marcie jogged 214 miles in June, 197 miles in July, and 84 miles in August. How many miles did she jog in the 3-month period?

  495 miles

NUMBER SENSE

15. Complete the numbers to form two 3-digit odd numbers and two 3-digit even numbers.

  7 5 1   2 9 3   3 8 2   6 6 4
  odd   odd   even   even

Use the numbers you wrote to solve. Write *odd* or *even* beside the difference.

  even   6 6 4
  − even − 3 8 2
  _____
  even   2 8 2

  even   6 6 4
  − odd − 2 9 3
  _____
  odd   3 7 1

  odd   7 5 1
  − odd − 2 9 3
  _____
  even 4 5 8

  odd   7 5 1
  − even − 1 0 0
  _____
  odd   6 5 1

Exploring Subtraction with Zeros

Use place-value models. Regroup to solve each problem. Choose **a, b,** or **c** to show how you regrouped.

1. 4 9 13
   503 ✓
   −258 ✓
   245

a.
H	T	O
4	10	13

b. (circled)
H	T	O
4	9	13

c.
H	T	O
3	9	10

2. 7 9 10
   800 ✓
   −349 ✓
   451

a.
H	T	O
7	10	10

b. (circled)
H	T	O
7	9	10

c.
H	T	O
8	9	10

3. 5 9 12
   602 ✓
   −498 ✓
   104

a.
H	T	O
5	10	12

b.
H	T	O
6	9	12

c. (circled)
H	T	O
5	9	12

4. 8 15 10
   960 ✓
   −386
   574

a. (circled)
H	T	O
8	15	10

b.
H	T	O
8	15	0

c.
H	T	O
8	16	10

5. 5 10 10
   610 ✓
   −492 ✓
   118

a.
H	T	O
6	9	10

b.
H	T	O
5	9	10

c. (circled)
H	T	O
5	10	10

MIXED REVIEW

Tell the value of the digit **7** in each number.

1. 47,819 ___7,000___ ✓   **2.** 703,124 ___700,000___ ✓

3. 1,798 ___700___ ✓   **4.** 670,253 ___70,000___ ✓

Multiply Using 2 as a Factor

Complete the multiplication sentence for each picture.

1.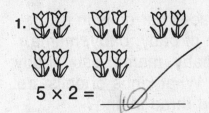

   5 × 2 = __10__

2.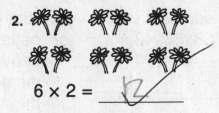

   6 × 2 = __12__

3.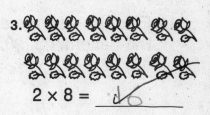

   2 × 8 = __16__

Write the multiplication sentence for each picture.

4.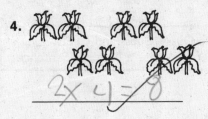

   __2 × 4 = 8__

5.

   __7 × 2 = 14__

6.

   __3 × 2 = 6__

Find the product. You may draw a picture or use a number line.

7.
   2
   × 5
   ___
   10

8.
   9
   × 2
   ___
   18

9.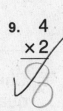
   4
   × 2
   ___
   8

10.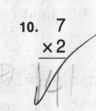
    7
    × 2
    ___
    14

11.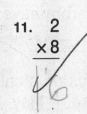
    2
    × 8
    ___
    16

12.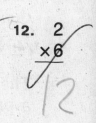
    2
    × 6
    ___
    12

Mixed Applications

Write a number sentence. Solve.

13. Sal has 6 rosebushes. He picks 2 roses from each bush. How many roses does he pick?

    __2 × 6 = 12__

14. Sal buys 24 pansies, 36 begonias, and 48 violas. How many flowers does Sal buy?

    __108 flowers__

LOGICAL REASONING

15. Luci, Juana, and Marco collect postcards when they go on trips. Luci has 3 fewer postcards than Juana. Marco has collected 5 postcards on each of 2 different trips. Juana has 2 times as many postcards as Marco. How many postcards does each person have?

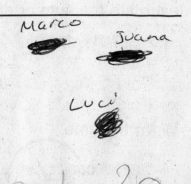

Luci has 17 postcards, Juana has 20 postcards and Marco 10

Problem-Solving Strategy
Find a Pattern

1. Find the next three numbers in the pattern: 23, 28, 33, 38, 43, 48, 53, _58_, _63_, _68_.

_____

2. Rita places her dolls in a pattern of baby, baby, mama, baby, baby, mama, baby, baby, mama. What kinds of dolls are the next three in line?

baby, baby, mama

Mixed Applications → **STRATEGIES**

• Act It Out • Guess and Check
• Find a Pattern • Write a Number Sentence

Choose a strategy and solve.

3. Barbra has 3 dolls. Each doll has 5 outfits. How many outfits does Barbra have for her dolls?

15 outfits

4. Draw the next five shapes in the pattern.

□□□○○□□□○○

5. The days on a calendar make a pattern. If May 4 is a Wednesday, what day of the week is May 11?

May 11 is a Wednesday

6. Chico has one $1 bill and one quarter. How much money does Chico have? Can he buy a lunch that costs $1.20?

$1.25 Yes he can

MIXED REVIEW

Round each number to the nearest hundred and estimate the sum or difference.

1. 397 _400_
   +215 _200_
   _600_

2. 413 _400_
   −295 _300_
   _100_

3. 683 _700_
   +106 _100_
   _800_

4. 209 _200_
   − 84 _100_
   _100_

5. 828 _800_
   +861 _900_
   _1,000_

Write the time.

6. _12:45_

7.  _9:19_

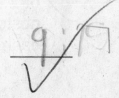

62

Multiply Using 3 as a Factor

Use the number line to find the product.

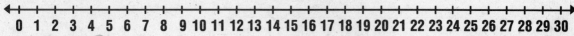

1. $3 \times 8 = $ 24

2. $4 \times 3 = $ 12

3. $3 \times 6 = $ 18

Write the multiplication sentence for each picture.

4.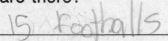

   $3 \times 4 = 12$

5. $7 \times 3 = 21$

6. $9 \times 3 = 27$

Find the product.

7. $\begin{array}{r} 2 \\ \times 3 \\ \hline \end{array}$ 6

8. $\begin{array}{r} 9 \\ \times 3 \\ \hline \end{array}$ 27

9. $\begin{array}{r} 3 \\ \times 8 \\ \hline \end{array}$ 24

10. $\begin{array}{r} 7 \\ \times 3 \\ \hline \end{array}$ 21

11. $\begin{array}{r} 3 \\ \times 5 \\ \hline \end{array}$ 15

12. $\begin{array}{r} 3 \\ \times 6 \\ \hline \end{array}$ 18

Mixed Applications

13. There are 5 shelves of footballs in a closet. Each shelf has 3 footballs. How many footballs are there?

    15 footballs

14. Kiri hunts lost golf balls. She finds 16 balls near the clubhouse. She finds 6 in one sandtrap, 9 in another trap, and 10 in the bushes. How many golf balls did she find?

    41 golf balls

    16
    6
    9
    10.

VISUAL THINKING

Draw number lines to help you solve.

15. José and Edward each filled a photo album. Edward said he had more photos than José because his album had 4 pages more than José's. José said he had more photos because he put 6 photos on each of the 5 pages in his album and Edward put 4 on each page. Which boy was right? How many photos did each boy have?

    $6 \times 5 = 30$
    ph pg
    ph

    4 pages more

    $9 \times 4 = 36$

    Jose has 10 photos and Edward has a photos.

    Edward

Multiply Using 4 as a Factor

Draw a picture for each multiplication sentence.
Solve.

1. 8 × 4 = _32_

2. 2 × 4 = _8_

3. 7 × 4 = _28_

Find the product.

4. 8
  ×3
  _24_

5. 3
  ×9
  _27_

6. 2
  ×4
  _8_

7. 7
  ×4
  _28_

8. 4
  ×9
  _36_

9. 3
  ×7
  _21_

10. 3 × 3 = _9_

11. 4 × 6 = _24_

12. 4 × 4 = _16_

13. 4 × 5 = _20_

Mixed Applications

14. Mabel buys 6 cards with animal buttons on them. Each card has 4 buttons. How many animal buttons does Mabel buy?

   24 buttons

15. Jen sews animal buttons on her clothes. She puts 4 tigers on her shirt, 3 giraffes on her hat, 16 seals on her skirt, and 1 lion on each glove. How many animal buttons does she sew?

   24 buttons

EVERYDAY MATH CONNECTION

In our money system, four quarters equal one dollar. Tell how many quarters equal each group of dollars.

 =

16. $2 = _8_ quarters

17. $3 = _12_ quarters

18. $4 = _16_ quarters

Multiply Using 5 as a Factor

Draw a picture for each multiplication sentence.
Solve.

1. 4 × 5 = 20

2. 3 × 5 = 15

3. 6 × 5 = 30

 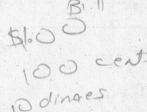 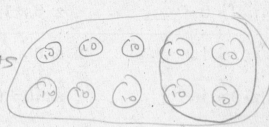

Find the product.

4. 8 × 5 = 40

5. 2 × 5 = 10

6. 7 × 5 = 35

7. 5 × 5 = 25

8. 5
   ×9
   45

9. 7
   ×4
   28

10. 5
    ×1
    5

11. 8
    ×3
    24

12. 9
    ×4
    36

13. 4
    ×5
    20

Write + , – ,or × for each ◯ .

14. 5 ⊕ 3 = 8

15. 5 ⊗ 3 = 15

16. 5 ⊖ 3 = 2

Mixed Applications

17. Jiro needs 5 nickels to pay for a pack of baseball cards. Write a multiplication sentence to find the cost. 5×5 = 25

18. Milo gave the clerk a $1 bill. The clerk gave Milo 4 dimes in change. How much change did Milo get? How much was his purchase? Milo got 40 dimes.

NUMBER SENSE

Solve the number puzzles.

19. One of my factors is 5. My product is 30. What is my other number? 5×6=30

20. My factors are both the same. My product is 25. What are my factors? 5×5=25

65

Multiply Using 1 and 0 as Factors

Find the product.

1. $9 \times 0 = $ _0_

2. $8 \times 1 = $ _8_

3. $4 \times 0 = $ _0_

4. $7 \times 1 = $ _7_

5. $6 \times 0 = $ _0_

6. $3 \times 1 = $ _3_

7. $9 \times 1 = $ _9_

8. $10 \times 0 = $ _0_

9. $8 \times 0 = $ _0_

10. $10 \times 1 = $ _10_

11. $7 \times 0 = $ _0_

12. $6 \times 1 = $ _6_

13. $\begin{array}{r} 4 \\ \times 0 \\ \hline 0 \end{array}$

14. $\begin{array}{r} 3 \\ \times 1 \\ \hline 3 \end{array}$

15. $\begin{array}{r} 2 \\ \times 0 \\ \hline 0 \end{array}$

16. $\begin{array}{r} 9 \\ \times 0 \\ \hline 0 \end{array}$

17. $\begin{array}{r} 1 \\ \times 1 \\ \hline 1 \end{array}$

18. $\begin{array}{r} 0 \\ \times 8 \\ \hline 0 \end{array}$

19. $\begin{array}{r} 5 \\ \times 1 \\ \hline 5 \end{array}$

20. $\begin{array}{r} 3 \\ \times 0 \\ \hline 0 \end{array}$

21. $\begin{array}{r} 4 \\ \times 1 \\ \hline 4 \end{array}$

22. $\begin{array}{r} 2 \\ \times 0 \\ \hline 0 \end{array}$

23. $\begin{array}{r} 0 \\ \times 5 \\ \hline 0 \end{array}$

24. $\begin{array}{r} 1 \\ \times 2 \\ \hline 2 \end{array}$

Mixed Applications

25. Marie put 1 sticker on each page of her 8-page sticker album. How many stickers did Marie put in her album?

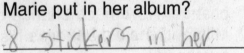

8 stickers in her album

26. Inez has 37 fuzzy stickers and 61 scented stickers. How many more scented stickers than fuzzy stickers does Inez have?

24 scented stickers

$\begin{array}{r} 5\llap{6}1 \\ -37 \\ \hline 24 \end{array}$

MIXED REVIEW

Write each number in standard form.

1. four hundred twenty-three thousand, sixteen   _____

2. ninety-seven thousand, one hundred thirty   _____

3. $800,000 + 40,000 + 600 + 30 + 1$ _____

4. $200,000 + 2,000 + 20$ _____

Problem Solving
Choose a Strategy

Mixed Applications ⟶	STRATEGIES	• Act It Out • Make a Model • Work Backward • Write a Number Sentence

Choose a strategy and solve.

1. Hector covered a wall using 1-foot mirror squares. The wall is 3 feet wide and 7 feet long. How many 1-foot squares did Hector use?

   21 1-foot squares

2. Abby made a tapestry design out of 16 square fabric samples. The design is in the shape of a square. Make a model of the design. Draw your model in the space below.

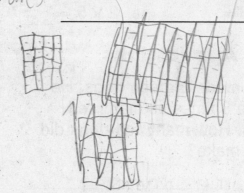

3. A large window is made up of square panes. The window is 4 panes wide and 8 panes long. How many panes make up the large window?

   _____

4. Mae, Sue, Bob, and Pete each bought a 5-sticker sheet. How many stickers did they have among them?

   _____

5. Tani spent 45 minutes in the mall. He left the mall at 2:30. At what time did he arrive at the mall?

   _____

WRITER'S CORNER

6. Write a problem that can be solved using the *Make a Model* strategy.

   _____

   _____

Mental Math:
Reviewing Facts 0–5

Find the product.

1. 4
   ×3
   ___
   12

2. 3
   ×7
   ___
   21

3. 5
   ×2
   ___
   10

4. 7
   ×2
   ___
   14

5. 8
   ×3
   ___
   24

6. 2
   ×9
   ___
   18

7. 4
   ×8
   ___
   32

8. 5
   ×5
   ___
   25

9. 3
   ×3
   ___
   9

10. 6
    ×2
    ___
    12

11. 2
    ×8
    ___
    16

12. 6
    ×3
    ___
    18

13. 2 × 6 = 12

14. 3 × 9 = 27

15. 4 × 5 = 20

16. 5 × 3 = 15

17. 5 × 6 = 30

18. 2 × 5 = 10

19. 3 × 4 = 12

20. 9 × 5 = 45

Mixed Applications

21. Wes made 2 green rings. He made 3 times as many red rings. How many red rings did Wes make?

    6 red rings

22. The Craft Shop sells 5 times as many red mats as blue. The shop sold 4 blue mats today. How many red mats were sold?

    20 mats were sold

23. Yarn is on sale for 5¢ a skein. How much will 9 skeins cost?

    45 ¢

24. Moe buys 48 shells. Joy buys 15 shells more than Moe. How many shells does Joy buy?

    63 shells

     48
    + 15
    ____
     63

VISUAL THINKING

Write the multiplication fact for each picture.

25.

    3×4=12

26.

    6×2=12

68

Connecting Subtraction and Division

Use the pictures to solve.

1.

How many twos
are in 8? _____

8 ÷ 2 = _____

2.

How many fives
are in 15? _____

15 ÷ 5 = _____

3.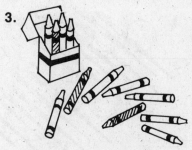

How many fours
are in 12? _____

12 ÷ 4 = _____

4. Draw 10 boxes.

Show 10 ÷ 2 = _____

5. Draw 6 chips.

Show 6 ÷ 3 = _____

6. Draw 12 sticks.

Show 12 ÷ 2 = _____

Mixed Applications

7. Ed has 8 pens. He puts them into groups of 2. Draw a picture to show how many groups of 2 pens Ed has.

8. Anna uses 1 eraser for every 2 packs of pencils she uses. If she uses 10 packs of pencils in a year, how many erasers will she use?

_____

WRITER'S CORNER

9. Write a few sentences describing one way to explain to a friend how to solve 18 ÷ 3.

_____

_____

_____

Connecting Multiplication and Division

Use the pictures to solve.

1.

$3 \times 7 =$ _____
$21 \div 7 =$ _____

2.

$5 \times 4 =$ _____
$20 \div 4 =$ _____

Write the fact family for each set of numbers.

3. 4, 6, 24

_____

_____

4. 2, 5, 10

_____

_____

5. 3, 9, 27

_____

_____

Mixed Applications

6. There are 18 students in Rosa's class. They are working in groups of 3. Draw a picture to show how many groups there are.

7. Some crayons are divided equally among 3 students. Each student gets 8 crayons. How many crayons are there?

_____

SCIENCE CONNECTION

Farmers in Pennsylvania have been feeding their cows chocolate to make their milk better. Each cow's daily feed includes about 4 pounds of chocolate. Tell how many cows could be fed with the following amounts of chocolate.

8. 8 pounds feeds _____ cows

9. 12 pounds feeds _____ cows

10. 24 pounds feeds _____ cows

11. 20 pounds feeds _____ cows

Dividing by 2
Using Addition Doubles

Find the quotient.

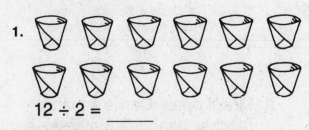

1. 12 ÷ 2 = _____

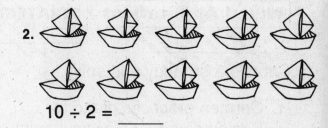

2. 10 ÷ 2 = _____

Find the missing factor.

3. 2 x _____ = 6   4. 2 x _____ = 10   5. _____ x 2 = 12   6. 9 x _____ = 18

Find the quotient.

7. 8 ÷ 2 = _____   8. 4 ÷ 2 = _____   9. 12 ÷ 2 = _____   10. 16 ÷ 2 = _____

11. 18 ÷ 2 = _____   12. 10 ÷ 2 = _____   13. 6 ÷ 2 = _____   14. 14 ÷ 2 = _____

Mixed Applications

15. Kim earned $3 an hour for raking leaves. It took him 2 hours to do the job. How much money did he earn?

_____

16. The dividend is 12. The divisor is 2. What is the quotient?

_____

MIXED REVIEW

Find the product.

1. 8
   ×3

2. 9
   ×7

3. 3
   ×8

4. 5
   ×9

5. 7
   ×8

6. 4
   ×6

Write the money amount.

7.  _____

8.   _____

Problem Solving
Choose a Strategy

| Mixed Applications > | STRATEGIES | • Act It Out • Guess and Check
• Draw a Picture
• Write a Number Sentence |

Choose a strategy and solve.

1. Carmen practices piano for 5 minutes a day. For how many minutes does she practice in a 6-day period?

_____

2. Mrs. Lopez, Carrie's piano teacher, teaches 3 classes a day, 5 days a week. How many classes does she teach in 5 days?

_____

3. Greg practices piano for 20 minutes a day. He plays each piece he is assigned for 5 minutes. How many pieces does he practice each day?

_____

4. Mrs. Lopez receives 12 roses from a student. She divides them equally among 4 vases. How many roses are in each vase?

_____

5. The piano recital is 4 weeks from today. In how many days is the recital?

_____

6. Tickets for the recital cost $6 for adults and $4 for children. How much will it cost for 2 adults and 3 children to go to the recital?

_____

MUSIC CONNECTION

A *duet* is a song played or sung by two musicians.
Tell the number of duets a class could play if there were

7. 6 students. _____

8. 10 students _____

9. 14 students. _____

10. 18 students _____

Dividing by 3

Write a division sentence for each.

1.

2.

_____

_____

Find the quotient.

3. $12 \div 3 =$ ____

4. $18 \div 3 =$ ____

5. $21 \div 3 =$ ____

6. $8 \div 2 =$ ____

7. $18 \div 2 =$ ____

8. $24 \div 3 =$ ____

9. $9 \div 3 =$ ____

10. $6 \div 3 =$ ____

Write × or ÷ for ◯ .

11. $15 \bigcirc 3 = 5$

12. $4 \bigcirc 2 = 8$

13. $9 \bigcirc 3 = 3$

14. $3 \bigcirc 7 = 21$

Mixed Applications

15. The checkers tournament began at 11:30. It ended 2 hours and 30 minutes later. At what time was it over?

_____

16. At the party after the tournament, Tom spent $0.65 for lemonade, $1.25 for a hot dog, and $0.95 for an apple. How much did Tom spend?

_____

VISUAL T_____

17. Connect the dots with 6 lines to make 2 squares. How many corners do the 2 squares have?

_____

18. Draw 3 more lines to make 6 triangles. How many corners do the 6 triangles have?

_____

Dividing by 4

Find the quotient.

1. $24 \div 4 =$ 6
2. $15 \div 3 =$ 5
3. $12 \div 2 =$ 6
4. $16 \div 4 =$ 4

5. $28 \div 4 =$ 7
6. $12 \div 4 =$ 3
7. $20 \div 4 =$ 5
8. $27 \div 3 =$ 9

9. $24 \div 3 =$ 8
10. $24 \div 4 =$ 6
11. $32 \div 4 =$ 8
12. $36 \div 4 =$ 9

13. $4 \overline{)12}$ 3
14. $4 \overline{)8}$ 2
15. $3 \overline{)9}$ 3
16. $2 \overline{)16}$ 8
17. $4 \overline{)24}$ 6
18. $3 \overline{)15}$ 5

19. $3 \overline{)21}$ 7
20. $4 \overline{)20}$ 5
21. $4 \overline{)28}$ 7
22. $2 \overline{)18}$ 4
23. $4 \overline{)32}$ 8
24. $4 \overline{)36}$ 9

Mixed Applications

25. The third-grade class used rhythm instruments in their show. Twenty four students shared 6 instruments. How many students shared each instrument?

    4 people shared each instrument

    $6 \overline{)24}$

26. The class sang 8 songs. Each song lasted about 2 minutes. How many minutes did all of the songs take?

    16 minutes

    $8 \times 2 = 16$

NUMBER SENSE

Study the tables. Then write *more* or *fewer* to complete each sentence.

Number of Toys for Each Child

Toys	3 Children	4 Children	6 Children
24	8	6	4

Number of Acorns for Each Squirrel

Squirrels	16 Acorns	12 Acorns	8 Acorns
4	4	3	2

27. If the number of toys stays the same, then the more children there are the fewer toys each child gets.

28. If the number of squirrels stays the same, then the fewer acorns there are the fewer acorns each squirrel gets.

Problem Solving
Choose the Operation

1. Terri schedules patients for Dr. Cruz to treat. She schedules 4 patients for a 1-hour period. Dr. Cruz works 7 hours a day. How many patients does Terri schedule for Dr. Cruz to see in a day?

28 people in 7 hours

2. Dr. Cruz works in a medical building. Altogether, 24 doctors work in the building. The building has 8 office spaces. An equal number of doctors use each office space. How many doctors work in each office space?

3 doctors

3. There are 6 doctors who share one large office in a medical building. Each doctor has 3 nurses who help with daily jobs. How many nurses work in the large office?

18 nurses

4. Joseph is now 51 inches tall. The doctor told Joseph that he had grown 5 inches since the last checkup. How tall was Joseph then?

46 inches

Mixed Applications	STRATEGIES	• Act It Out • Guess and Check • Work Backward • Find a Pattern

Choose a strategy and solve.

5. There are 4 children in the doctor's waiting room. Meg will be seen after Jo. Bee will be seen before Juan. Jo will be seen first. Meg will be seen before Bee. In what order will the children be seen?

Jo, Meg, Bee, Juan

6. Dr. Malone bought some new books for her office waiting room. For every 3 children's books she bought, she received 1 book for parents at no cost. If there were 16 books in the shipment, how many free parents' books did Dr. Malone receive?

4 parent books

91

Dividing by 7

Find the quotient.

1. $14 \div 7 = $ _____
2. $28 \div 7 = $ _____
3. $7 \div 7 = $ _____
4. $49 \div 7 = $ _____

5. $42 \div 7 = $ _____
6. $21 \div 7 = $ _____
7. $63 \div 7 = $ _____
8. $56 \div 7 = $ _____

9. $7\overline{)35}$
10. $7\overline{)14}$
11. $6\overline{)42}$
12. $7\overline{)28}$
13. $3\overline{)27}$
14. $7\overline{)56}$

15. $7\overline{)21}$
16. $6\overline{)36}$
17. $4\overline{)0}$
18. $6\overline{)24}$
19. $7\overline{)63}$
20. $7\overline{)7}$

Write × or ÷ in each ◯

21. $7 \bigcirc 9 = 63$
22. $42 \bigcirc 7 = 6$
23. $36 \bigcirc 6 = 6$
24. $8 \bigcirc 2 = 4$

Mixed Applications

25. Julio works at a plant nursery. He waters 1,234 flower plants, 217 bushes, and 48 trees. How many plants does Julio water in all?

   _____

26. Mr. Chu buys 9 mum plants. After careful rooting and replanting of these mums, Mr. Chu has 63 mums two years later. If an equal number came from each of the original mums, how many mums did he grow from each original plant?

   _____

SCIENCE CONNECTION

A plant gets water through its roots. Then the water moves up the stem to the leaves. In an experiment, a celery stalk was placed in red-colored water. Every hour, the red water traveled another 3 cm up the stalk.

27. How many hours did it take for the red water to travel 12 cm up the celery stalk?

   _____

28. If the stalk is 21 cm long, how many hours will it take for the water to travel from one end of the stalk to the other?

   _____

Dividing by 8

Find the missing factor.

1. $4 \times \underline{\hspace{1cm}} = 32$
2. $5 \times \underline{\hspace{1cm}} = 0$
3. $\underline{\hspace{1cm}} \times 9 = 63$
4. $8 \times \underline{\hspace{1cm}} = 48$

Find the quotient.

5. $7 \times 8 = 56$, so $56 \div 8 = \underline{\hspace{1cm}}$.
6. $3 \times 8 = 24$, so $24 \div 8 = \underline{\hspace{1cm}}$.

7. $5 \times 8 = 40$, so $40 \div 8 = \underline{\hspace{1cm}}$.
8. $9 \times 8 = 72$, so $72 \div 8 = \underline{\hspace{1cm}}$.

9. $2 \times 8 = 16$, so $16 \div 8 = \underline{\hspace{1cm}}$.
10. $0 \times 8 = 0$, so $0 \div 8 = \underline{\hspace{1cm}}$.

11. $8\overline{)24}$
12. $6\overline{)24}$
13. $5\overline{)40}$
14. $7\overline{)42}$
15. $8\overline{)56}$
16. $5\overline{)5}$

17. $4\overline{)36}$
18. $8\overline{)48}$
19. $4\overline{)32}$
20. $5\overline{)45}$
21. $8\overline{)72}$
22. $8\overline{)64}$

Mixed Applications

23. Ms. West's third grade is having a mathathon. Each student is asked to complete a 72-problem booklet in 8 days. Millie will do the same number of problems each day. How many problems will she do each day?

_____

24. Millie sees that 3 pages in the math booklet each have 9 addition problems, and 4 pages each have 7 subtraction problems. Are there more addition or more subtraction problems in the booklet?

_____

MIXED REVIEW

Find the sum or difference.

1.
```
  8,345
  2,468
     42
+   846
```

2.
```
  3,901
  1,023
      9
+ 2,497
```

3.
```
   809
 − 397
```

4.
```
  $89.26
   12.09
 +  7.95
```

5.
```
  $4.00
 − 1.56
```

Dividing by 9

Find the quotient.

1. $54 \div 9 =$ _____   2. $36 \div 9 =$ _____   3. $81 \div 9 =$ _____   4. $27 \div 3 =$ _____

5. $18 \div 9 =$ _____   6. $72 \div 8 =$ _____   7. $48 \div 6 =$ _____   8. $21 \div 7 =$ _____

9. $9\overline{)36}$ 10. $7\overline{)42}$ 11. $9\overline{)81}$ 12. $7\overline{)63}$ 13. $9\overline{)9}$ 14. $7\overline{)56}$

15. $8\overline{)48}$ 16. $9\overline{)45}$ 17. $9\overline{)0}$ 18. $9\overline{)63}$ 19. $6\overline{)54}$ 20. $9\overline{)27}$

Mixed Applications

21. The Springdale Sports Club has 63 students signed up for baseball teams. There are 7 equal-size teams formed. How many students are on each team?

_____

22. One baseball team collects $5 from each of its 9 players to buy the coach a gift. How much money is collected?

_____

23. One factor is 2 less than the other. The product is 48. What are the factors?

_____

24. In one game, Kristi scores 4 more runs than Jon. Jon scores 1 run fewer than Carlos. Carlos scores 3 runs. How many runs do Jon and Kristi each score?

_____

WRITER'S CORNER

25. Write a problem that you can solve by dividing by 9.

_____

_____

_____

_____

Lilyam

Exploring Solid Figures

Manipulatives

    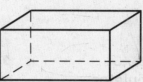

| Cube | Cone | Cylinder | Sphere | Rectangular Prism | Pyramid |

Name the figure that each looks like.

1.

Cylinder

2.

Sphere

3.

rectangular prism

4.

pyramid

5.

cube

6.

cone

Solve the riddle. Use your solid figures.

7. I have 5 faces. All but 1 are triangles. What am I?

pyramid

8. I have 6 faces. Only 2 are squares. What am I?

rectangular prism

WRITER'S CORNER

9. Write a riddle that has a solid figure as its answer.

I have 2 faces but it is a circle and all of my faces except 1 are triangles.

Exploring Plane Figures

Name the figure that each looks like.

1.

    scircle

2.

    square

3.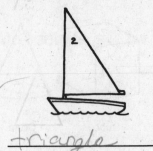

    triangle

4.

    pentiegon

5.

    circle

6.

    square

Draw a line from the description to the figure.

7. 4 sides and 4 corners
   All sides are the same length.

8. 4 sides and 4 corners
   All sides are not the same length.

9. 3 sides and 3 corners

10. 0 sides and 0 corners

11. 5 sides and 5 corners

rectangle

circle

pentagon

square

triangle

EVERYDAY MATH CONNECTION

Name two things in the kitchen of your home that are
shaped like each figure listed.

12. Square   oven   dishwasher

13. Rectangle   table   counter

14. Circle   plate   pot

98

Exploring Line Segments and Angles

Find the number of line segments in each figure.

1.

_____

2.

_____

3.

_____

Write whether each angle is a *right angle* or *less than* or *greater than* a right angle.

4.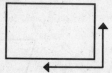

_____

5.

_____

6.

_____

Draw each figure.

7. I have 4 right angles. I have 4 sides. All are the same length.

8. I have 0 right angles. I have 6 sides. I have 6 angles.

EVERYDAY MATH CONNECTION

Each kind of road sign has a special shape. Write the word or words that might be written inside each sign.

9.

_____

10.

_____

11.

_____

Exploring Congruent Figures

Tell whether the two figures are congruent.
Write *yes* or *no*.

1.

Yes

2.

NO

3.

Yes

Ring the figure that is congruent to the shaded
figure.

4.

5.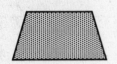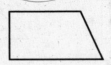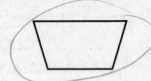

6.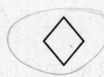

7. Write a sentence describing how you can tell
   whether two figures are congruent.

   I can tell by if they are both the same
   shape and size.

MIXED REVIEW

Solve.

1. $3 \times 5 = 15$ 2. $4 \times 8 = 32$ 3. $36 \div 9 = 4$ 4. $72 \div 8 = 9$

Find the quotient. Use counters to help you.

5. $\overset{4 R1}{3\overline{)13}}$ 6. $\overset{4 R2}{4\overline{)18}}$ 7. $\overset{2 R2}{5\overline{)12}}$ 8. $\overset{7 R1}{2\overline{)15}}$ 9. $\overset{1 R3}{6\overline{)9}}$

$\underline{-12}$ $\underline{-16}$ $\underline{-10}$ $\underline{-14}$ $\underline{-6}$

01 2 2 1 3

100

Exploring Symmetry

Trace the figure. Cut out your drawing and fold it in half. Write *yes* or *no* to tell whether the figure has a line of symmetry.

1.

_____

2.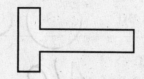

_____

3.

_____

Is the dotted line a line of symmetry? Write *yes* or *no*.

4.

_____

5.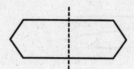

_____

6.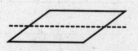

_____

Draw a line of symmetry.

7.

8.

9.

VISUAL THINKING

10. Draw an open figure.

11. Draw a closed figure.

Problem-Solving Strategy
Find a Pattern

1. Diego's schedule for practicing piano follows a pattern. He practices for 5 minutes on Monday, 8 minutes on Tuesday, 11 minutes on Wednesday, and 14 minutes on Thursday. For how many minutes does Diego practice on Friday? on Saturday?

   _____

   _____

2. Megan is saving her pennies for a new piano book. She saves 1 penny the first day. On the second day she saves 2 pennies, on the third day she saves 4 pennies, and on the fourth day she saves 8 pennies. How many pennies will she save on the fifth day? on the sixth day?

   _____

   _____

| **Mixed Applications** | **STRATEGIES** | • Guess and Check • Find a Pattern
• Write a Number Sentence • Draw a Picture |

Choose a strategy and solve.

3. It is 4:00 when Ned and Sue begin a math project. Ned finishes it in 15 minutes. Sue finishes 8 minutes later than Ned. At what time does Sue finish the math project?

   _____

4. Zack and Jack play a pattern game. Zack says 4, and Jack says 8. Zack says 5, and Jack says 10. Zack says 6, and Jack says 12. What does Jack say when Zack says 7? What does Jack say when Zack says 9?

   _____

VISUAL THINKING

5. Draw the two shapes that will come next.

Exploring Perimeter

Choose a book from your desk, classroom, or home.
Find its perimeter three times. Each time use a
different unit of measure. Use the units of measure in
the list below.

  a. width of your finger
  b. width of a pencil
  c. width of a paper clip

Complete the table.

	Unit of Measure	Guess	Perimeter
1.	Finger width	20	13
2.	Pencil width	4	4
3.	Clip width	75	30

Use the width of a crayon. Find the perimeter of
each figure.

4. _10_ units

5. _16_ units

6. _12_ units

7. _8_ units

CAREER CONNECTION

James is a carpenter. He is putting wood trim around
the window in a hallway. He needs to know the
perimeter of the window so that he can buy the
correct amount of wood.

8. Write a sentence describing how James could
   use a ruler to find the perimeter.

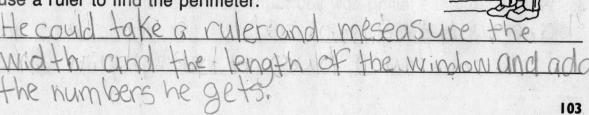

He could take a ruler and meseasure the
width and the length of the window and add
the numbers he gets.

103

Exploring Area

Fill in squares with your pencil. Make three shapes, each with an area of 6 square units.

1.

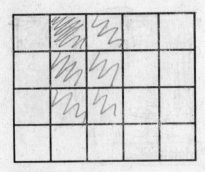

2.

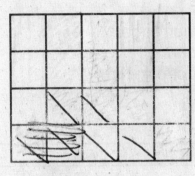

3.

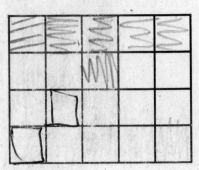

Find the area of each figure. Label your answer in square units.

4.

8 square units

5.

15 square units

6.

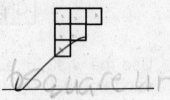

6 square units

7.

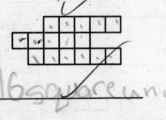

16 square units

8.

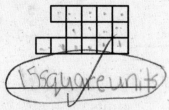

15 square units

9.

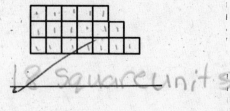

18 square units

VISUAL THINKING

The area of this figure is 4 square units.
Write the area of each figure below.

10.

8 square units

11.

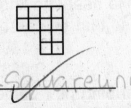

12 square units

12.

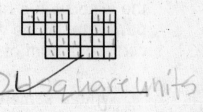

24 square units

13. Write a sentence telling how you found your answers.

The area is when you count how many squares are inside a shape thats how I got my answer

104

Exploring Volume

Manipulatives

Use cubes to build the shapes. Find the volume of each shape.

1.

8 cubic units

2.

12 cubic units

3.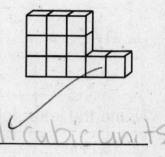

11 cubic units

4.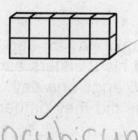

10 cubic units

5.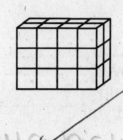

24 cubic units

6.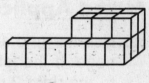

18 cubic units

7.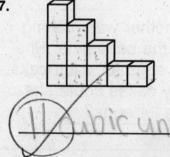

11 cubic units

8.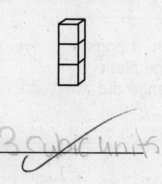

3 cubic units

9.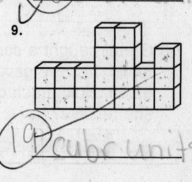

19 cubic units

MIXED REVIEW

Find the sum or difference.

1.	2.	3.	4.	5.
457 +398 855	689 −297 392	4,109 +2,863 6,972	$3.09 − 1.98 $1.11	$16.75 + 4.50 $21.25

Write × or ÷ for ◯ .

6. 8 Ⓧ 5 = 40   **7.** 72 ◯ 9 = 8   **8.** 45 ◯ 5 = 9   **9.** 6 Ⓧ 6 = 36

Using Points on a Grid

Write the ordered pair for each letter.

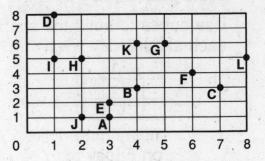

1. A ___   2. B ___   3. F ___   4. H ___

5. G ___   6. I ___   7. K ___   8. L ___

Name the letter for each ordered pair.

9. (3,2) ___   10. (7,3) ___   11. (2,1) ___   12. (1,8) ___

Mixed Applications

13. Use the grid at the top of the page. If the letter E is moved to the right 2 spaces and up 1 space, what word would you see?

_____

14. Yoshi's family has an egg farm. Yoshi and his 2 sisters each gathered 6 eggs one day. How many eggs did they gather in all?

_____

15. Gretel bought a carton of eggs for $1.17. She gave the clerk $2.00. How much change did she receive?

_____

16. Gretel's mother was making cakes for the bake sale. She needed 3 eggs for each cake. How many cakes could she make with 24 eggs?

_____

EVERYDAY MATH CONNECTION

Imagine the grid at the right is a map. Tell the location of these places.

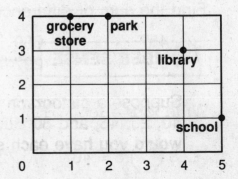

17. library ___   18. grocery store ___

19. school ___   20. park ___

Problem-Solving Strategy
Make a Pictograph

1. On which day were the fewest tickets sold?

   _____

2. How many more tickets were sold on Friday than on Thursday?

   _____

Number of Circus Tickets Sold	
Monday	🎟🎟🎟🎟🎟🎟
Tuesday	🎟🎟🎟🎟🎟
Wednesday	🎟🎟🎟🎟
Thursday	🎟🎟🎟🎟🎟🎟
Friday	🎟🎟🎟🎟🎟🎟🎟🎟
Saturday	🎟🎟🎟🎟🎟🎟🎟

Each 🎟 = 5 tickets

3. Make a pictograph of lunch choices for a third-grade class. There are 16 students who bring lunch, 8 students who buy hot lunch, and 12 students who buy cold lunch. Use ☺ to show students. Have 1 ☺ stand for 2 students.

   _____

   1 ☺ = 2 students

4. Write the title on the line above your graph.

Mixed Applications

5. In the pictograph above, Ernesto wants to make 1 ☺ stand for 4 students. How many ☺'s would he draw for bringing lunch?

   _____

6. The school sold 425 hot lunches on Monday. It sold 87 fewer hot lunches on Tuesday. How many hot lunches did it sell on Tuesday?

   _____

NUMBER SENSE _____

7. Suppose a pictograph is to show classes of 35, 40, 20, 45, and 30 students. How many students would you have each symbol stand for? Explain.

_____

Exploring Length
Inch

Manipulatives

Measure the length of each in inches.

1.  _____

2. 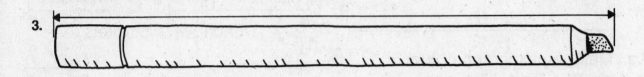 _____

3. _____

Draw each length from the •.

4. 2 inches •

5. 1 inch •

6. 4 inches •

7. Find two things in your home that measure about 9 inches each.

_____

Mixed Applications

8. Marcy's ribbon is 12 inches long. She cuts a 9-inch piece to tie into a bow. How much ribbon is left?

9. Jorge connects 2-inch paper clips to make a chain. How long is Jorge's chain if he uses 5 paper clips?

_____

LOGICAL REASONING

10. Yoshi glues his report to a piece of colored paper. The report paper is 8 inches wide and 10 inches long. The colored paper makes a 1-inch border around the report paper. How wide is the colored paper?

_____

Length
Foot, Yard, and Mile

Ring the better estimate.

1. the length of a piece of paper

   11 inches or 11 feet

2. the length of a football field

   100 feet or 100 yards

3. the length of your classroom

   20 yards or 20 miles

4. the distance from your home to school

   2 yards or 2 miles

5. the height of your chair

   2 feet or 2 yards

6. the distance a car travels

   20 yards or 20 miles

Mixed Applications

7. Jeremiah buys tomato plants for his garden. He spaces them 18 inches apart. How many inches from the first plant is the third plant? Draw a picture.

   _____

8. Jeremiah's garden is a rectangle that measures 2 feet long and 6 feet wide. What is the perimeter of the garden?

   _____

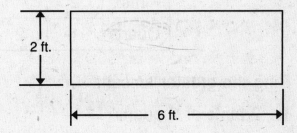

SCIENCE CONNECTION

9. A potato plant grows to a height of 4 inches within two weeks of planting. It then grows another inch every 3 days. In how many days from planting will the potato plant be 10 inches tall?

   _____

Exploring Capacity
Customary Units

Ring the better estimate.

1. (1 quart) or 1 gallon

2. 1 pint or (1 gallon)

3. 5 pints or (5 gallons)

4. 1 cup or (1 quart)

Tell which unit of measure you would use. Write *c, pt, qt,* or *gal.*

5. milk in a glass

   about 1 _c_

6. water in an aquarium

   about 10 _gal_

7. water in a cooler

   about 4 _gal_

8. juice in a small carton

   about 1 _pt_

Complete the table.

9.

Cups	4	8	12	16	20	24
Pints	2	4	6	8	10	12
Quarts	1	2	3	4	5	6

Ring the greater amount.

10. 2 pints or (2 quarts)

11. (8 cups) or 2 pints

12. (4 pints) or 1 quart

13. 4 cups or (2 quarts)

NUMBER SENSE

14. Pepita is making punch for the school party. She wants 1 pint of sherbet for every 2 quarts of juice. Pepita has 2 gallon jugs of apple juice and 2 quart cartons of cranberry juice. How many pints of sherbet does Pepita need?

Exploring Weight
Ounce and Pound

Which unit of measure would you use to weigh each item? Write *ounce* or *pound*.

1. pound

2.  pound

3.  pound

4. 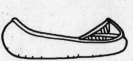 pound

Ring the better estimate.

5. **1 pound**
   or
   1 ounce
   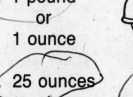

6. **8 ounces**
   or
   8 pounds

7. **25 ounces**
   or
   25 pounds
   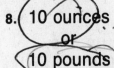

8. **10 ounces**
   or
   10 pounds

Solve.

9. A can with 3 tennis balls weighs 14 ounces. Do the tennis balls weigh *more than* or *less than* 1 pound?

   More

10. Su-Lyn wears 2 wrist weights that weigh 12 ounces each. What is the total weight of the wrist weights?

    24

less

MIXED REVIEW

Find the product or quotient.

1. $4 \times 9 = 36$

2. $72 \div 8 = 9$

3. $8 \times 7 = 56$

4. $14 \div 7 = 2$

5. $7\overline{)63}$ 9

6. $9\overline{)72}$ 8

7. $3\overline{)24}$ 9

8. $5\overline{)40}$ 8

9. $9\overline{)18}$ 2

10. $6\overline{)6}$

Exploring Fahrenheit Temperature

Ring the more reasonable temperature.

1. hot soup

   50°F or (120°F)

2. sledding party

   (30°F) or 80°F

3. swimming party

   15°F or (85°F)

Write each temperature.

4.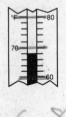

   68°

5.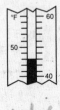

   46°

6.

   80°

7.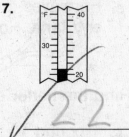

   22°

Mixed Applications

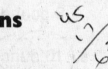

Solve.

8. When Ruth woke up, the thermometer read 45°F. Two hours later the temperature had risen 17°. What was the temperature then?

   62°F

9. A fan will go on if the temperature goes above room temperature. Will the fan go on if the thermometer reads 50°F?

   no

EVERYDAY MATH CONNECTION

Draw a line to match the temperature on each thermometer to the right clothes that should be worn.

10.

11.

12.

13.

Problem Solving
Choose a Strategy

Mixed Applications > STRATEGIES	• Write a Number Sentence • Act It Out • Draw a Picture • Guess and Check

Choose a strategy and solve.

1. Keith is swimming in the middle lane of the pool. He waves to Juan, who is 3 lanes away, in the end lane. How many lanes does the pool have?

_____

2. Lian has 36-inch shoelaces. After lacing her shoes, she finds that there are 10 inches on each end for tying. How many inches are used to lace the shoes?

_____

3. Members of the swim team lined up in order from shortest to tallest. There were 6 people behind Paula. There were 13 swimmers in all. How many people were in front of Paula?

4. Paula bought a team swimsuit for $22.75, a swim cap for $5.50, and goggles for $4.95. She also spent $15.00 on team membership. What was Paula's total cost to join the swim team?

LOGICAL REASONING

5. There are 8 people in a line. Maria is at the front of the line. There are 3 people between Maria and Jeff. Max is behind Jeff. There is one person between Max and Jeff. What is Max's position in line?

_____

Exploring Length
Centimeter

Manipulatives

Measure the length of each in centimeters.

1.

_____

2.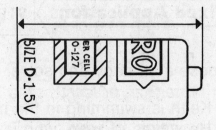

_____

Draw each length from the •.

3. 2 centimeters •

4. 3 centimeters •

5. 12 centimeters •

Solve.

6. When Sofia tapped the golf ball, it moved 35 centimeters. It is still 17 centimeters from the hole. How far was the ball from the hole before Sofia tapped it?

_____

7. The yellow golf ball is 16 centimeters from the hole. The red golf ball is 7 centimeters closer. How far is the red golf ball from the hole?

_____

LOGICAL REASONING

A crayon measures about 8 centimeters. A crayon can be used to estimate lengths of other objects. Measure the objects using an 8-centimeter crayon. Then multiply by 8 to find the approximate length.

	crayons	centimeters
8. the length of your math book	_____	_____
9. the length of a pencil	_____	_____
10. the height of your chair	_____	_____

Exploring Length
Meter and Kilometer

Ring the better estimate.

1. the length of a chalkboard

   8 meters or 80 meters

2. the height of a child

   1 meter or 5 meters

Is it *more* than or *less* than a meter?

3. the height of your chair

   more   less   than 1 meter

4. the height of a door

   more   less   than 1 meter

Is it *more* than or *less* than a kilometer?

5. the distance that an airplane flies

   more   less   than a kilometer

6. the distance from your chair to the school office

   more   less   than a kilometer

Complete each sentence. Write *cm, m,* or *km.*

7. Hannah's jump rope is about 1 _____ long.

8. The distance around the playground is about 2 _____ .

9. A baseball bat is about 85 _____ long.

Solve.

10. Jared can run 1 kilometer in about 8 minutes. How long will it take him to run 7 kilometers?

    _____

11. In the softball toss, Abby threw distances of 28 meters and 37 meters. What is the combined distance?

    _____

| HEALTH CONNECTION |

12. Here are Olympic running events. Ring the events whose distances are 1 kilometer or greater.

    100-meter run   200-meter run   400-meter run   800-meter run

    1,000-meter run   1,500-meter run   10,000 meter run

Capacity
Milliliter and Liter

Choose the unit you would use to measure each.
Write *milliliter* or *liter*.

1. water in a thimble

_____

2. milk in a cup

_____

3. orange juice in a jug

_____

Ring the better estimate.

4.

2 mL or 2 L

5.

250 mL or 250 L

6.

6 mL or 6 L

Mixed Applications

7. Henry filled his cat's 500-mL water dish this morning. Now the dish has 175 mL of water. How much did the cat drink?

_____

8. A small can of juice contains 650 mL. The large can holds 1,000 mL. How many more mL does the large can of juice hold?

_____

9. Yoko combines 875 mL of white paint and 250 mL of red paint. Does Yoko make *more* than or *less* than 1,000 mL of pink paint?

10. A 25-L pot of soup is divided equally into 5 smaller containers for storage. How much soup does each container hold?

WRITER'S CORNER

11. Make a list of foods, liquids and household items that may come in containers holding about 1 liter.

Food _____

Liquids _____

Household Items _____

Exploring Weight
Gram and Kilogram

Which unit of measure would you use to weigh each item? Write *gram* or *kilogram*.

1. an envelope

2. a crayon

3. a desk

_____   _____   _____

Complete each sentence. Write *grams* or *kilograms.*

4. Vic's dog weighs about 10 _____.

5. The dog's bone weighs about 65 _____.

Use the graph for Exercises 6–8.

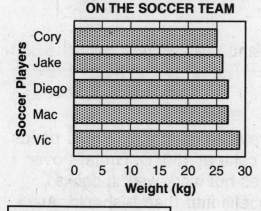

WEIGHT OF SOME PLAYERS ON THE SOCCER TEAM

6. Which student weighs the most?

_____

7. Which students are the same weight?

_____

8. Write Cory's and Jake's weight.

_____

MIXED REVIEW

Find the sum or difference.

1. $4.25
   + 1.79

2. $18.97
   + 10.75

3. 600
   − 236

4. 4,290
   +2,175

5. 8,125
   − 1,023

Ring the figures that are congruent to the first one.

6.

Exploring Celsius Temperature

Ring the more reasonable temperature.

1. hot cereal

   – 30°C or (90°C)

2. ice cube

   20°C or (0°C)

3. picnic weather

   20°C or (80°C)

4. room temperature

   20°C or (70°C)

5. swimming weather

   – 30°C or (30°C)

6. frozen yogurt

   20°C or (– 5°C)

Write each temperature.

7.

   12°

8.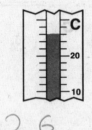

   26°

9.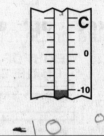

   -10°

Solve.

10. Edgar must increase the oven temperature by 15°C every half hour for a science project. He started at 90°C at 1:30 P.M. What should the temperature be at 3:00 P.M.?

    135°

11. Gretel bakes bread. Bread needs to bake at 150°C. Gretel's oven does not work well. It cooks 20°C hotter than it should. At what temperature should Gretel set her oven?

    130°

LOGICAL REASONING

12. In Newton the temperature is 11°C. In <u>Shannon</u> the temperature is 20°C higher than in Newton.
    In <u>Las Palos</u> it is 10°C colder than in Shannon.
    In <u>Richmond</u>, it is 5°C warmer than in Las Palos.
    List the cities from lowest to highest temperatures.

    Newton, Las Palos, Richmond, Shannon

Problem Solving
Use a Bar Graph

Use the bar graph for Exercises 1–2.

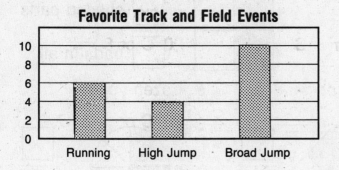

Favorite Track and Field Events

1. Which event is the favorite?

_____

2. How many more students voted for the broad jump than for the high jump?

_____

Mixed Applications | **STRATEGIES** | • Act It Out • Draw a Picture • Write a Number Sentence • Work Backward

Choose a strategy and solve.

3. Della's soccer ball was reduced from $9.50 to $7.97. How much money did Della save by buying the ball at the reduced price?

_____

4. Juanita measures her new tennis racket. The stringed head is 9 inches. The handle is 11 inches. What is the racket's length?

_____

5. A square field measures 6 yards on each side. What is the perimeter of the field?

_____

6. On Saturday, Tad jogged from 1:55 until 2:40. For how long did Tad jog?

_____

VISUAL THINKING

7. Mr. Ming may swim the perimeter of Pool A or Pool B. In which pool must he swim farther? How much farther?

_____

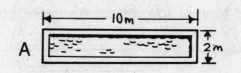

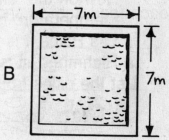

Exploring Fractions

Write the fraction for the part that is shaded.
Then say the fraction.

1. $\dfrac{4}{5}$ shaded parts / parts in all

2. $\dfrac{2}{4}$ shaded parts / parts in all

3. 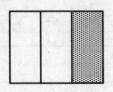 $\dfrac{1}{3}$

4. 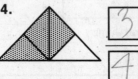 $\dfrac{3}{4}$

5. $\dfrac{5}{8}$

Write the fraction for the part that is shaded.

6. 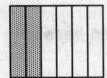 $\dfrac{2}{6}$

7. $\dfrac{4}{5}$

8. $\dfrac{4}{4}$

Write the fraction for each word name.

9. one third $\dfrac{1}{3}$

10. two fifths $\dfrac{2}{5}$

11. four sixths $\dfrac{4}{6}$

EVERYDAY MATH CONNECTION

Many foods must be divided into fractional parts in order for people to share them. Shade one fourth of each food item to show one serving out of four.

12.

13.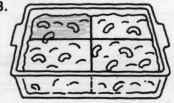

14.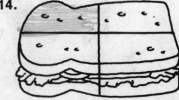

Exploring Part of a Group

Write the fraction for the part that is shaded. Tell if each shows *part of a whole* or *part of a group*.

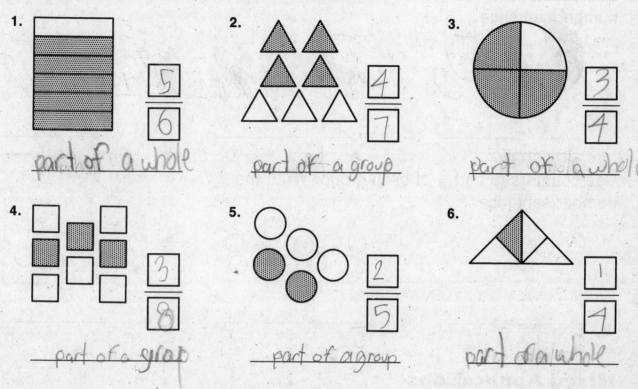

1. $\dfrac{5}{6}$ part of a whole

2. $\dfrac{4}{7}$ part of a group

3. $\dfrac{3}{4}$ part of a whole

4. $\dfrac{3}{8}$ part of a grop

5. $\dfrac{2}{5}$ part of a group

6. $\dfrac{1}{4}$ part of a whole

Write the fraction that names the part of the group described.

7. boxes with bows $\dfrac{3}{8}$

8. Polka dot ribbons $\dfrac{2}{5}$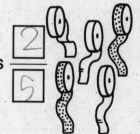

SCIENCE CONNECTION

Evelyn planted flower seeds all around her garden.

Shade the flowers that bloomed in Evelyn's garden.

9.

Three sevenths are red.
Four sevenths are blue.

10.

Five eighths are orange.
Three eighths are yellow.

Finding Part of a Group

Manipulatives

Use counters to find $\frac{1}{3}$ of each group. Write the number sentence.

1.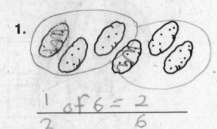

$\dfrac{1}{3}$ of $6 = \dfrac{2}{6}$

2.

$\dfrac{1}{3}$ of $12 = \dfrac{4}{12}$

3.

$\dfrac{1}{3}$ of $9 = \dfrac{3}{9}$

Use counters to find $\frac{1}{5}$ of each group. Write the number sentence.

4.

$\dfrac{1}{5}$ of $5 = \dfrac{1}{5}$

5.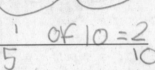

$\dfrac{1}{5}$ of $10 = \dfrac{2}{10}$

6.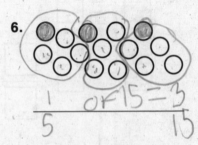

$\dfrac{1}{5}$ of $15 = \dfrac{3}{15}$

Mixed Applications

7. Sam bought 12 apples. He used $\frac{1}{4}$ of them to make an apple pie. How many apples did Sam use?

Sam used 3 apples to make an apple pie.

8. Ruth had $4. She spent $\frac{1}{2}$ of her money on lunch. How much money did she have left?

Ruth had 2 dollars left.

VISUAL THINKING

9.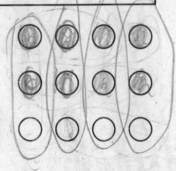

How many circles are there? __12 circles__

How many circles are in $\frac{1}{3}$ of the group?

$\dfrac{4}{12}$

To find the circles in $\frac{2}{3}$ of the group, you count the number in 2 out of 3, or $\frac{2}{3}$ of the rows. How many circles are in $\frac{2}{3}$ of the group?

$\dfrac{8}{12}$

122

Exploring Equivalent Fractions

Write *true* or *false*.

1.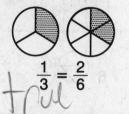

$\frac{1}{3} = \frac{2}{6}$

true

2.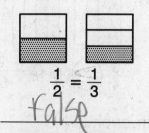

$\frac{1}{2} = \frac{1}{3}$

false

3.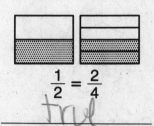

$\frac{1}{2} = \frac{2}{4}$

true

4.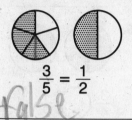

$\frac{3}{5} = \frac{1}{2}$

false

5.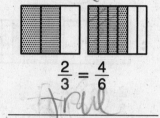

$\frac{2}{3} = \frac{4}{6}$

True

6.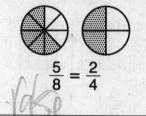

$\frac{5}{8} = \frac{2}{4}$

false

Name the equivalent fraction.

7.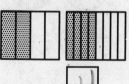

$\frac{2}{4} = \frac{4}{8}$

8.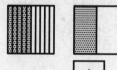

$\frac{5}{10} = \frac{1}{2}$

9.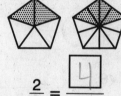

$\frac{2}{5} = \frac{4}{10}$

10.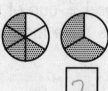

$\frac{4}{6} = \frac{2}{3}$

11.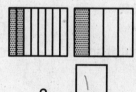

$\frac{2}{8} = \frac{1}{4}$

12.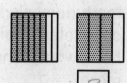

$\frac{6}{8} = \frac{3}{4}$

MIXED REVIEW

Find the product or quotient.

1. $\begin{array}{r} 5 \\ \times 3 \\ \hline 15 \end{array}$

2. $\begin{array}{r} 8 \\ \times 5 \\ \hline 40 \end{array}$

3. $\begin{array}{r} 7 \\ \times 7 \\ \hline 49 \end{array}$

4. $\begin{array}{r} 4 \\ \times 9 \\ \hline 36 \end{array}$

5. $\begin{array}{r} 9 \\ \times 6 \\ \hline 54 \end{array}$

6. $\begin{array}{r} 0 \\ \times 2 \\ \hline 0 \end{array}$

7. $4\overline{)32}$

8. $5\overline{)45}$

9. $4\overline{)28}$ 7

10. $8\overline{)48}$

11. $6\overline{)36}$

Exploring Comparing Fractions

Compare. Write < or > in each ◯.

1.

$\frac{1}{3}$ ◯ $\frac{2}{3}$

2.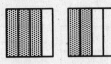

$\frac{3}{4}$ ⬲ $\frac{2}{4}$

3.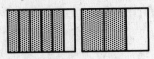

$\frac{5}{6}$ ◯ $\frac{2}{3}$

Compare. Write <, >, or = in each ◯.

4.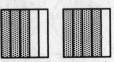

$\frac{3}{5}$ ◯ $\frac{4}{5}$

5.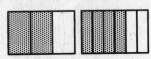

$\frac{2}{3}$ ◯ $\frac{4}{6}$

6.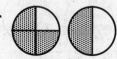

$\frac{3}{4}$ ◯ $\frac{1}{2}$

7.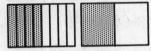

$\frac{4}{8}$ ◯ $\frac{1}{2}$

8.

$\frac{3}{5}$ ◯ $\frac{3}{8}$

9.

$\frac{2}{5}$ ◯ $\frac{4}{5}$

Solve.

10. Quint has finished $\frac{2}{5}$ of his math homework. Greta has completed $\frac{2}{3}$ of the same homework. Who has completed more?

Greta has completed more homework than Quint.

11. A bowl of muffin batter contains $\frac{1}{3}$-cup of oil and $\frac{2}{3}$-cup of milk. Do the muffins have more *milk* or more *oil*?

the muffins have more milk than oil.

WRITER'S CORNER

12. Two pizzas are equal in size. One is cut into 6 equal pieces. The other is cut into 8 equal pieces. Which pizza has larger pieces? Explain your answer.

The pizza that has 6 pieces has bigger pieces than the other pizza because in factors the more greater numbers you have the less amount of pieces you have.

Mixed Numbers

Draw a picture to show the mixed number.

1. Draw 4 rectangles.
   Color $3\frac{1}{5}$ rectangles yellow.

2. Draw 2 rectangles.
   Color $1\frac{4}{4}$ rectangles green.

Use the ruler. Choose the best answer. Ring **a**, **b**, or **c**.

3. Two and one-eighth inches is closest to _____ inches.

   a. 1   b. 2   c. 3

4. One and seven-eighths is closest to _____ inches.

   a. 1   b. 2   c. 3

Complete the pattern.

5. $\frac{1}{4}$, $\frac{2}{4}$, $\frac{3}{4}$, 1, $1\frac{1}{4}$, $1\frac{2}{4}$, _____ , _____ , _____

Mixed Applications

6. Marta ate $\frac{1}{6}$ of a pie.
   Yoki ate $\frac{2}{6}$ of a pie.
   Who ate more?

   _____

7. At closing time Mr. Pizza still had $2\frac{7}{8}$ unsold pizzas. Is this closer to *2 pizzas* or *3 pizzas*?

   _____

VISUAL THINKING

8. Write the mixed number that names the shaded part. Order the numbers from least to greatest.

   _____

   _____   _____   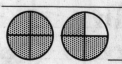 _____

Exploring Probability

Look at the spinner. Write the correct answer.

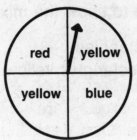

1. What are the chances that the pointer will stop on red?

   _____

2. What are the chances that the pointer will stop on yellow? _____

3. On which color is the spinner most likely to stop? Why? _____

What are the chances of picking an orange? Ring **a** or **b**.

4.    **a.** 1 out of 4

                                 b. 1 out of 5

5.    **a.** 1 out of 4

                                 b. 2 out of 4

Suppose you drop a cube several times on each gameboard.

A.    B. 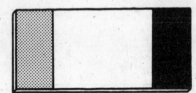   C.

6. On which board is a cube most likely to land on white? Why?

   _____

7. On which board is a cube least likely to land on black? Why?

   _____

8. Which board is a fair board? Why? _____

VISUAL THINKING

9. Color the circles in the bag. Make the chances of drawing

   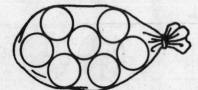

   red: 1 out of 7.   yellow: 3 out of 7.
   green: 1 out of 7.   blue: 2 out of 7.

126

Problem-Solving Strategy
Draw a Picture

Solve. Use the strategy *draw a picture.*

1. At Harry's Uniform Shop, $\frac{1}{2}$ of the uniforms are red, $\frac{2}{5}$ are blue, and $\frac{3}{10}$ are gold. Of which color uniform does Harry have the most?

2. Harry sells 15 gold uniforms. He has matching helmets for only $\frac{1}{3}$ of the uniforms. How many helmets is he missing?

_____

Mixed Applications ➤ | **STRATEGIES** | • Guess and Check • Draw a Picture • Act It Out • Find a Pattern

Choose a strategy and solve.

3. A carousel ride costs $4 for adults and $3 for children. Mr. Sanchez pays $23 for 7 people. For how many adults does he pay? How many children?

_____

4. A gameboard has 27 squares. Each square is red or blue. The number of red squares is two times the number of blue squares. How many squares of each color are there?

_____

WRITER'S CORNER

5. Write a problem about this picture.

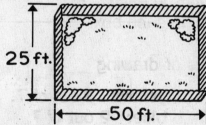

25 ft.   50 ft.

_____

_____

_____

_____

Decimals

Tenths

Write the decimal for the part that is shaded.

1.

0.7

2.

0.1

3.

0.4

Write each fraction as a decimal.

4. $\frac{2}{10}$ 0.2

5. $\frac{5}{10}$ 0.5

6. $\frac{9}{10}$ 0.9

7. $\frac{3}{10}$ 0.3

Write each decimal as a fraction.

8. 0.4 $\frac{4}{10}$

9. 0.8 $\frac{8}{10}$

10. 0.1 $\frac{1}{10}$

11. 0.6 $\frac{6}{10}$

Mixed Applications

Write each answer as a fraction and as a decimal.

12. In one tennis match, Chris won 6 out of 10 games. What part of the games did Chris win?

$\frac{6}{10}$ 0.6

13. Jaime served the ball 10 times. He scored a point on his serve 3 of those times. On what part of his serves did Jaime score a point?

$\frac{3}{10}$ 0.3

NUMBER SENSE

14. Write each as a decimal. Then order the decimals in each set from the least to greatest. Write *1, 2, 3,* or *4* in each box.

$\frac{3}{10}$ 0.3 [2]

$\frac{2}{10}$ 0.2 [1]

seven tenths   0.7 [4]

five tenths   0.5 [3]

Decimals
Hundredths

Write the decimal that tells what part is shaded.

1. _0.20_

2. _0.37_ 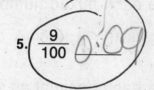 _0.09_

Write each fraction as a decimal

3. $\frac{83}{100}$ _0.83_

4. $\frac{48}{100}$ _0.48_

5. $\frac{9}{100}$ _0.09_

Write each decimal as an amount of money.

6. forty-five hundredths _$0.45_

7. sixty-two hundredths _$0.62_

Use the place-value chart for Exercises 8–9.

8. In 0.56, what digit is in the hundredths place? _6_

9. In 0.34, in what place is the digit 0? _ones_

Ones	.	Tenths	Hundredths
0	.	5	6
0	.	3	4

Mixed Applications

10. Marcy spent 60 cents on a pen and 10 cents on an eraser. Write the amount that Marcy spent as a decimal and as a dollar amount.

    _0.70 $0.70_

11. Mr. Quest had 100 squiggle pencils to sell. He sold 30 of them in one hour. Write the number of pencils sold as a fraction and a decimal.

    $\frac{30}{100}$ 0.30

LOGICAL REASONING

12. How would a place-value chart show decimal parts of a dollar? Complete the chart headings.

1 dollar		Dimes	Pennies
$ 1	.	0	0

_1.08_   _1.80_

129

Decimals Greater Than 1

Write a decimal for the part that is shaded.

1. 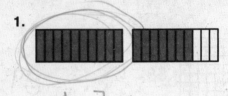   2.   3.

_1.7_   _3.5_   _2.26_

0.7

Write each mixed number as a decimal.

4. $6\frac{7}{10}$ _6.07_   5. $12\frac{72}{100}$ _12.72_   6. $27\frac{4}{100}$ _1.04_

Write each decimal as a mixed number.

7. 4.3 $4\frac{3}{10}$ 8. 9.03 $9\frac{3}{100}$ 9. 67.29 $67\frac{29}{100}$

Write each decimal in words.

10. 4.7 _four point seven_

11. 8.92 _eight wholes point ninety-two out of one-hundred_

Mixed Applications

12. Fred bought a toy bat and ball for $3.17. The bat cost $1.98. How much was the ball?

_____

13. Susan and Jeff each had a dollar. Susan spent $\frac{1}{2}$ of her dollar. Jeff spent $\frac{3}{4}$ of his dollar. Who spent more?

Jeff spent more

WRITER'S CORNER

14. Explain how you can tell that 0.3 is equal to 0.30.

Because in both of them you shade in 3 bars

Decimals
Adding and Subtracting

Find the sum or difference.

1. 3.4
   +2.5

2. 2.6
   +3.7

3. 2.5
   +5.5

4. 3.19
   +4.56

5. 4.10
   +2.88

6. 5.9
   −2.5

7. 9.1
   −1.9

8. 8.1
   −6.3

9. 8.15
   −5.90

10. 6.00
    −4.50

11. 1.9
    +7.9

12. 7.2
    −4.5

13. 3.72
    +5.25

14. 9.35
    −3.28

15. 7.88
    +1.45

Mixed Applications

16. The daytime temperature one day was 72.8 degrees. The temperature dropped 23.5 degrees by nightfall. What was the temperature then?

_____

17. Sam ran the 10-kilometer race in 53.25 minutes. It took Ed 49.80 minutes to run the same race.

a. Who ran faster? _____

b. How much faster? _____

MIXED REVIEW

Write the temperature shown in degrees Celsius.

1.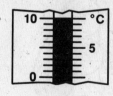

_____

2.

_____

3.

_____

Write the missing number.

4. 9 × _____ = 63

5. 4 × _____ = 32

6. 81 ÷ _____ = 9

7. 48 ÷ _____ = 8

8. 16 ÷ _____ = 4

9. 5 × _____ = 45

Problem Solving
Multistep Problems

1. There were 4 cans of tennis balls with 3 balls in each can. Luis and Jane lost 7 balls. How many are left?

_____

2. Mona played tennis with Jill from 9:30 until 10:15. She played with Rita from 2:45 until 3:35. For how long did Mona play tennis?

_____

Mixed Applications ➤ **STRATEGIES**
- Write a Number Sentence
- Guess and Check • Work Backward
- Draw a Picture

Choose a strategy and solve.

3. There are 12 muffins on a baker's rack. Of these, $\frac{1}{3}$ are blueberry muffins and $\frac{1}{2}$ are bran muffins. How many blueberry muffins are there? How many bran muffins?

_____

4. Sean bought a basketball for $12.88 and a football for $9.75. How much more did the basketball cost?

_____

VISUAL THINKING

Bag A    Bag B

5. From which bag are you more likely to draw a shaded marble? Explain by telling the chances of getting a shaded marble in each case.

It would be more likely to pick a shaded marble from bag B because it has 2 shaded marbles and bag A has 1 marble.

Exploring Multiplying Tens and Hundreds

Manipulatives

Copy and complete. Use mental math or place-value materials to help you.

1. $3 \times 7 = 3 \times 7$ _____ = _____ ones = 21

   $3 \times 70 = 3 \times 7$ _____ = _____ tens = _____

   $3 \times 700 = 3 \times 7$ _____ = _____ hundreds = _____

2. Since $3 \times 3 = 9$, $3 \times 30 =$ _____, and $3 \times 300 =$ _____

3. Since $5 \times 7 = 35$, $5 \times 70 =$ _____, and $5 \times 700 =$ _____

4. $4 \times 3 =$ _____   5. $3 \times 9 =$ _____   6. $6 \times 5 =$ _____

   $4 \times 30 =$ _____ $3 \times 90 =$ _____ $6 \times 50 =$ _____

   $4 \times 300 =$ _____ $3 \times 900 =$ _____ $6 \times 500 =$ _____

7. $\begin{array}{r} 50 \\ \times\ 4 \\ \hline \end{array}$
8. $\begin{array}{r} 400 \\ \times\ 9 \\ \hline \end{array}$
9. $\begin{array}{r} 30 \\ \times\ 5 \\ \hline \end{array}$
10. $\begin{array}{r} 80 \\ \times\ 7 \\ \hline \end{array}$
11. $\begin{array}{r} 900 \\ \times\ 6 \\ \hline \end{array}$

VISUAL THINKING

Write multiplication number sentences to describe the pictures.

12.

13.

14.

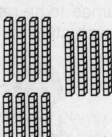

_____   _____   _____

Exploring Multiplying Two-Digit Numbers

Manipulatives

Find the total. Use place-value materials to help you.

1. 4 groups of 15 = _____

2. 3 groups of 24 = _____

3. 3 groups of 16 = _____

4. 2 groups of 37 = _____

Find the product. Use place-value materials to help you.

5. 3 × 13 = _____   6. 5 × 15 = _____   7. 2 × 28 = _____   8. 8 × 12 = _____

9. 4 × 16 = _____   10. 2 × 43 = _____   11. 3 × 25 = _____   12. 4 × 18 = _____

13. two times twenty-nine = _____

14. four times thirty-one = _____

15. The students in each of 4 classes at Andian School recycled 27 foam lunch trays on Monday. How many trays did they recycle on Monday?

16. Foam lunch trays cost George's school about 2¢ each. How much money does the school save by recycling 27 lunch trays?

_____   _____

CONSUMER CONNECTION

Recycling centers around the country pay 5¢ for every aluminum can or bottle returned to be recycled. Find the total amount earned by each student.

17.

18.

19.

_____   _____   _____

Multiplying Two-Digit Numbers
Manipulatives

Find the product. Use place-value materials to help you.

1. 27
   × 2
   54

2. ²18
   × 3
   54

3. 42
   × 2
   84

4. ¹38
   × 2
   76

5. ³17
   × 5
   85

6. ³19
   × 4
   76

7. 23
   × 4
   92

8. 34
   × 2
   68

9. 16
   × 5
   80

10. 22
    × 4
    88

11. 25
    × 3
    75

12. 18
    × 2
    36

13. 18 × 4 = 72

14. 28 × 3 = 84

15. 13 × 5 = 65

16. 4 × 13 = 52

17. 3 × 24 = 72

18. 5 × 16 = 80

Mixed Applications

19. A senator receives 2 letters a day from students who support the Clean Air Bill. How many letters does the senator receive in a 31-day month?

    62

20. Ms. Dey's class checked the temperature 3 times a day. How many readings would they collect at the end of a 4-week period?

    12

EVERYDAY MATH CONNECTION

George works at an electric plant. He earns $9 an hour. How much money does he earn in a:

21. 35-hour work week?

    315   315

    35
    × 9

22. 30-hour work week?

    270

23. 20-hour work week?

    180

    9 × 20 =

24. 45-hour work week?

    45
    × 9
    405

Regrouping Ones and Tens

Manipulatives

Find the product. Use place-value materials to help you.

1. 63
    × 2

2. 42
    × 3

3. 83
    × 2

4. 36
    × 4

5. 71
    × 5

6. 52
    × 4

7. 12
    × 8

8. 34
    × 5

9. 31
    × 6

10. 33
    × 4

11. 42
    × 4

12. 28
    × 6

13. 4 × 45 = _____

14. 3 × 39 = _____

15. 3 × 72 = _____

Mixed Applications

16. Teri works at a recycling center. She earns $8 an hour. How much money does she earn in a 35-hour work week?

17. The center received 5,102 cans in March and 3,574 cans in April. How many more cans did the center receive in March than in April?

MIXED REVIEW

Solve.

1.

   $\frac{1}{4}$ of 12 = _____

2.

   $\frac{1}{3}$ of 15 = _____

3. 4.2
    + 5.8

4. 9.7
    − 1.9

5. 3.45
    + 2.73

6. 4.15
    − 0.97

7. 8.95
    − 2.71

Multiplying Three-Digit Numbers

Find the product.

1. 103
   × 8

2. 215
   × 3

3. 141
   × 7

4. 274
   × 2

5. 225
   × 4

6. 150
   × 5

7. 342
   × 5

8. 468
   × 2

9. 591
   × 4

10. 412
    × 8

11. 154
    × 6

12. 807
    × 3

13. 360
    × 3

14. 903
    × 5

15. 223
    × 4

16. 649
    × 2

17. 164
    × 5

18. 650
    × 7

19. 6 × 145 = _____

20. 7 × 24 = _____

21. 5 × 112 = _____

Mixed Applications

22. There are 112 acres in each section of a wildlife preserve. How many acres are in 7 sections?

    _____

23. Each ticket to a national park costs $5.75. How much money do 4 tickets cost?

    _____

NUMBER SENSE

24. Write a multiplication problem in which you do not need to regroup. How did you choose your numbers? Explain.

    ×

    _____

    _____

    _____

    _____

    _____

Estimating Products

Estimate by rounding. Tell whether the estimate is *greater* than or *less* than your exact answer.

1. 37 × 4	2. 91 × 3	3. 53 × 5	4. 780 × 6	5. 305 × 8	6. 419 × 7
_____	_____	_____	_____	_____	_____

Estimate using front digits. Tell whether the estimate is *greater* than or *less* than your exact answer.

7. 83 × 3	8. 49 × 2	9. 215 × 4	10. 573 × 7	11. 188 × 9	12. 720 × 6
_____	_____	_____	_____	_____	_____

Mixed Applications

13. A recycling center can process 930 pounds of paper each day. Estimate how many pounds can be processed in 5 days.

14. A large barrel holds 72 pounds of used paper. About how many pounds of paper would 6 barrels hold?

WRITER'S CORNER

15. Look at Exercises 1–6. When is your estimate greater than the actual product? When is it less than the actual product? Write a sentence to explain.

_____

_____

_____

Problem-Solving Strategy
Use Estimation

Solve. Use estimation.

1. A watering can costs $6.35. A shovel costs $4.55. A spade costs $3.15. Estimate the total cost for all three items.

_____

2. Tickets for a ride cost $4.05 for adults and $2.15 for children. Estimate how much two adults and three children would pay.

_____

Mixed Applications > **STRATEGIES** •Write a Number Sentence • Act It Out • Work Backward • Draw a Picture

Choose a strategy and solve.

3. Scouts are planting maple trees at the bottom of Climb Hill. They plant oak trees nearer the top of the hill than the spruce trees. Pine trees are planted at the top of the hill. In what order are the trees planted from top to bottom?

_____

4. Hip Heating promises a savings of $15.50 on your monthly electric bill if you set your thermostat at 62 degrees each night. The Wu family's bill was $89.35 with Hip. What would they have paid if they had not used Hip?

SCIENCE CONNECTION

At the San Diego Zoo, animals eat about 225 pounds of barley, 79 pounds of seeds, and 55 bushels of apples in one week.

About how much food does the San Diego Zoo need for each time period? Estimate by rounding.

	Time Period	Barley (pounds)	Seeds (pounds)	Apples (bushels)
5.	2 weeks			
6.	4 weeks			
7.	8 weeks			

Exploring Division Patterns

Show the quotients on the place-value chart.

Place-Value Chart

	Hundreds	Tens	Ones
1. 8 ÷ 4

80 ÷ 4

800 ÷ 4

Place-Value Chart

	Hundreds	Tens	Ones
2. 20 ÷ 5

200 ÷ 5

2,000 ÷ 5

Use mental math to find the quotient.

3. 4)‾80‾

4. 2)‾60‾

5. 6)‾360‾

6. 5)‾250‾

7. 7)‾350‾

8. There were 120 people at the rally. They arrived in 3 buses. Each bus held the same number of people. How many people were on each bus?

_____

9. Carlos mailed 320 fliers. He mailed the same number of fliers on each of 4 days. How many fliers did Carlos mail each day?

_____

VISUAL THINKING

How much money will each person receive if each group of ten-dollar bills is divided evenly among 4 people? Write a number sentence.

10.

11.

12.

_____   _____   _____

_____   _____   _____

Exploring Quotients with Remainders

Manipulatives

Use your counters. Find the quotient.

1. 3)28   2. 4)32   3. 5)27   4. 8)35   5. 2)17

6. 9)83   7. 8)47   8. 6)37   9. 7)49   10. 4)39

11. 8)42   12. 4)19   13. 9)60   14. 7)58   15. 5)45

16. 7)25   17. 5)29   18. 9)29   19. 8)43   20. 9)37

MIXED REVIEW

Identify each figure.

1.

2.

3.
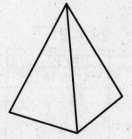

_____ _____ _____

Compare the numbers. Write <, >, or = in the ◯ .

4. 78 ◯ 87   5. 193 ◯ 193   6. 5,222 ◯ 5,227

7. 7,031 ◯ 7,310   8. 1,140 ◯ 920   9. 35,190 ◯ 25,198

Find the sum.

10. $1.15
  + 1.15

11. $5.09
  + 3.26

12. $2.67
  + 1.93

13. $3.22
  + 6.06

14. $8.45
  + 4.81

Exploring Two-Digit Quotients with Remainders

Find the quotient. Use your place-value materials.
Then check each answer by using multiplication.

1. 47 ÷ 3   3)47

Check:

2. 35 ÷ 2   2)35

Check:

3. 53 ÷ 4   4)53

Check:

4. 55 ÷ 2   2)55

Check:

5. 58 ÷ 3   3)58

Check:

6. 69 ÷ 5   5)69

Check:

7. 29 ÷ 2   2)29

Check:

8. 52 ÷ 3   3)52

Check:

9. 75 ÷ 4   4)75

Check:

VISUAL THINKING

10. Write a division problem and its multiplication
check for this example.

Problem Solving
Choose a Strategy

Mixed Applications → **STRATEGIES**
- Find a Pattern
- Guess and Check
- Work Backward
- Draw a Picture
- Write a Number Sentence

Choose a strategy and solve.

1. Tamara finished her homework at 4:15. She had been working for 45 minutes. What time did she begin her homework?

_____

2. Mrs. Edgar reviewed the math homework. Tamara got $\frac{1}{5}$ of the 20 math exercises wrong. How many were correct?

_____

3. Ramón and Stan were playing a game. Ramón said 10, Stan said 15. Ramón said 25, Stan said 30. Ramón said 50, Stan said 55. What did Stan say when Ramón said 85?

_____

4. Jules and Jordan collected 24 cans for the recycling drive. Jules collected twice as many as Jordan. How many cans did Jules and Jordan collect?

_____

WRITER'S CORNER

5. Write a problem using information from the bar graph. Solve.

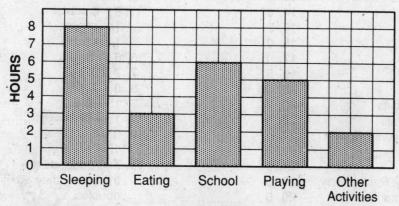

_____

_____

_____

_____

_____

Core Skills: Math, Grade 3, Answer Key

Page 1
1. 8
2. 11
3. 11
4. 12
5. 15
6. 11
7. 13
8. 14
9. 13
10. 11
11. 12
12. 10
13. 12
14. 12
15. 9
16. 11
17. 16
18. 10
19. 15
20. 10
21. 15 fish
22. 8 rainbow fish
23. bottom number line
24. top number line
25. middle number line

Page 2
1. 6
2. 15
3. 15
4. 13
5. 17
6. 5
7. 9
8. 10
9. 13
10. 11
11. 4
12. 15
13. 11
14. 12
15. 13
16. 11
17. 8
18. 17
19. 14
20. 14
21. 16
22. 13
23. 18
24. 16
25. 9
26. 14
27. 10
28. 12
29. 15
30. 12 oz

31. 10 months old
32. Answers will vary.
    Possible answers:
    6, 10, 4, 12, 14
33. Answers will vary.
    Possible answers:
    15, 17, 13, 11, 9

Page 3
1. 5
2. 6
3. 8
4. 16
5. 9
6. 7
7. 12, 12
8. 14, 14
9. 12, 12
10. 7 + 8 = 15
11. 4 + 9 = 13
12. 7 fish
13. 10 penguins
14. Answers will vary.

Page 4
1. 12
2. 14
3. 12
4. 18
5. 12
6. 11
7. 13
8. 11
9. 15
10. 15
11. 18
12. 13
13. 17
14. 17
15. 13
16. 13
17. 17
18. 18
19. 15
20. 11
21. 18
22. 15
23. 15
24. 8 robins
25. 13 pets
26. Answers will vary.

Page 5
1. Gary, Pablo, Perry,
   Herman
2. cheetah, horse,
   cat, dog
3. in front

4. 15 dogs
5. Answers will vary.

Page 6
1. 3
2. 4
3. 4
4. 7
5. 2
6. 7
7. 1
8. 3
9. 3
10. 3
11. 5
12. 1
13. 1
14. 5
15. 2
16. 2
17. 7
18. 5
19. 2
20. 1
21. 5 kittens
22. 3 more cans
23. 5¢, 6¢, 4¢

Page 7
1. 0
2. 9
3. 8
4. 10
5. 3
6. 6
7. 0
8. 5
9. 1
10. 9
11. 9
12. 0
13. 7
14. 6
15. 8
16. 0
17. 0
18. 5
19. 0
20. 8
21. 1
22. 5
23. 8
24. 0
25. 5
26. 0
27. 7
28. 0 kittens
29. 9 pets

30. –
31. –
32. +
33. –
34. +
35. +
36. –
37. +
38. –

Page 8
1–12. Possible answers
      are given.
1. 15 – 8 = 7
2. 15 – 6 = 9
3. 12 – 3 = 9
4. 17 – 9 = 8
5. 11 – 5 = 6
6. 14 – 7 = 7
7. 8 + 8 = 16
8. 7 + 6 = 13
9. 6 + 9 = 15
10. 8 + 4 = 12
11. 3 + 8 = 11
12. 9 + 5 = 14
13. 15 monkeys
14. 4 bananas
15. Number sentences
    will vary.

Page 9
1. 4, 8, 12
2. 6, 7, 13
3. 7 + 8 = 15,
   8 + 7 = 15,
   15 – 8 = 7,
   15 – 7 = 8
4. 9 + 4 = 13,
   4 + 9 = 13,
   13 – 4 = 9,
   13 – 9 = 4
5. 6 + 8 = 14,
   8 + 6 = 14,
   14 – 6 = 8,
   14 – 8 = 6
6. 6, 9, 6, 9
7. 7 + 8 = 15
8. 8 + 7 = 15,
   15 – 8 = 7,
   15 – 7 = 8
9. 6 + 6 = 12;
   12 – 6 = 6
10. The addends are
    the same; they are
    doubles.

Core Skills: Math, Grade 3, Answer Key (cont.)

Page 10
1. 7
2. 9
3. 6
4. 8
5. 9
6. 9
7. 4
8. 5
9. 9
10. 6
11. 3
12. 8
13. 7
14. 7
15. 9
16. 8
17. 2
18. 6
19. 5 miles
20. 7 dogs
Mixed Review
1. 13
2. 14
3. 6
4. 8
5. 0
6. 14
7. 18
8. 8
9. 8

Page 11
1. +
2. −
3. −
4. −
5. +
6. +
7. −
8. −
9. −
10. +
11. +
12. −
13. −
14. −
15. +
16. 9 treats
17. 9 weeks
18. Answers will vary.

Page 12
1. Cathy, 8 gerbils;
   Juanita, 6 gerbils
2. noon, 6 minutes;
   after dinner,
   9 minutes

3. fish book, $7;
   bird magazine, $9
4. 11 lionheads;
   6 fantails
5. Sally is first.
   Bill is last.
6. 7 chickens
7. Possible answer:
   If it was too low,
   I tried using higher
   numbers (and vice
   versa).

Page 13
1. even
2. odd
3. odd
4. even
5. odd
6. even
7. 20, 50, 60
8. 25, 15, 10
9. 29, 31, 35
10. 20, 30
11. 21, 25, 29, 33, 37,
    41, 45, 49
12. 29, 35, 37
13. Ring 1, 3, 5, 7, 9,
    11, and 13 in red;
    and ring 2, 4, 6, 8,
    10 and 12 in blue.
    Blue. Blue and red
    (even and odd)
    numbers alternate.
    Since 13 is red
    (odd), the next
    number would
    be blue.

Page 14
1. 723
2. 109
3. 475
4. 316
5. 579
6. 740
7. 485
8. 610
9. 34, 234
10. 356, 556
11. 772, 972
12. 407, 607
13. 4
14. 15
15. 683
16. 947

Page 15
1. <
2. >
3. >
4. =
5. <
6. >
7. <
8. >
9. >
10. =
11. <
12. <
13. >
14. <
15. Ninety-three is
    greater than eighty-
    eight.
16. Vicki
17. Bud
18. Salt Lake City
19. San Francisco

Page 16
1. 80, 83, 87
2. 31, 35, 38
3. 92, 94, 96
4. 246, 251, 297
5. 803, 830, 897
6. 505, 550, 555
7. 373, 341, 337
8. 698, 689, 675
9. 762, 750, 726
10. 515, 510, 501
11. 432, 430, 423
12. 970, 957, 907
13. more
14. east; 100 miles
Mixed Review
1. 13
2. 15
3. 6
4. 8
5. 14
6. 9
7. 6
8. 6
9. 7

Page 17
1. 40
2. 80
3. 90
4. 60
5. 30¢
6. 50¢
7. 60¢

8. 90¢
9. 50
10. 60¢
11. 20
12. 50¢
13. 83, 78, 75
14. 71¢, 65¢, 67¢, 69¢
15. 5, 6, 7, 8, 9, 10,
    11, 12, 13, 14
16. 45, 54
17. 21, 22, 23, or 24
    pounds
18. pen, memo pad,
    diary

Page 18
1. 800
2. 700
3. 700
4. 800
5. 600
6. 300
7. 800
8. 900
9. 300
10. 500
11. 200
12. 500
13. 350
14. 850
15. 650
16. 11 people
17. 400 people
18. Rounding to the
    nearest ten is
    usually more
    accurate. Since ten
    has a lesser value,
    the estimate is
    usually closer to
    the actual number.

Page 19
1. Police Station
2. Fire Station
3. Civic Center
4. 5 field trip ideas
5. Votes recorded will
   vary.
6. Answers will vary.

Page 20
1. 87
2. 432
3. 905
4. 4,707
5. 6,024
6. 7,145
7. 2,001
8. $1,427
9. Sue
10. $3,045
11. c

Page 21
1. >
2. >
3. >
4. >
5. <
6. =
7. 2,345; 12,123; 22,486
8. 23,676; 32,076; 32,570
9. 68,921; 69,129; 70,291
10. 99,099; 99,900; 99,909
11. Map A
12. 147,046 square miles
13. 31,700; 23,000; 22,300; 9,910; 7,550

Page 22
1. 500
2. 5,000
3. 50,000
4. 500,000
5. 232,074
6. 70,820
7. 32,096; 41,096; 131,096
8. 250,861; 259,861; 349,861
9. 891,421; 900,421; 990,421
10. 622,940; 631,940; 721,940
11. 275,000
12. Hoa; 3 more
13. 990,421

Page 23
1. 20
2. 35
3. D

4. G
5. L
6. thirteenth
7. ten
8. fifth
9. Ring nd.
10. Ring st.
11. Ring rd.

Page 24
1. Check table.
2. Week 8
3. Week 3
4. Week 7, Week 1, Week 8
5. Ana
6. $3.25
7. 2,143
8. 3,143
9. 2,043

Page 25
1. 50 + 20 = 70
2. 20 + 70 = 90
3. 90 − 40 = 50
4. 90 + 50 = 140
5. 70 − 30 = 40
6. 60 + 100 = 160
7. 40 + 70 = 110
8. 60 − 20 = 40
9. 80 reptiles
10. 20 posters
Mixed Review
1. 38,471
2. 406,935
3. 54,723
4. 730,403
5. 1,759; 1,900; 2,030
6. 3,898; 4,115; 4,657

Page 26
1. 80
2. 100
3. 100
4. 90
5. 80
6. 40
7. 60
8. 30
9. 60
10. 50
11. 90
12. 60
13. 77
14. 81
15. 75
16. 73
17. 32

18. 69
19. 90
20. 81
21. 91
22. 98
23. 91
24. 80
25. 80 minutes
26. 27 pieces
27. George; $0.05

Page 27
1. 90
2. 100
3. 100
4. 100
5. 120
6. 140
7. 105
8. 151
9. 106
10. 122
11. 107
12. 119
13. 114
14. 125
15. 134
16. 78
17. 127
18. 146
19. 120
20. 78
21. 145
22. 58
23. 126
24. 65
25. 52 minutes
26. 174 fish
27. less than
28. greater than

Page 28
1. 20 + 20 + 40 = 80
2. 50 + 20 + 30 = 100
3. 80 + 20 + 30 = 130
4. 30 + 40 + 40 = 110
5. 138
6. 152
7. 106
8. 141
9. 135
10. 107
11. 97
12. 111
13. 6 shows; 16 shows
14. 48 dogs, horses, and tigers
15. 124

16. 134
17. 144
18. 149
19. 174
20. 179
21. The sum is 100 more than the number, less 1.

Page 29
1. b
2. a; 102 acres
3. a; 86 pages
4. b
5. 6 times
6. 16 years
7. Answers will vary.

Page 30
1. 100 − 30 = 70
2. 50 − 20 = 30
3. 80 − 40 = 40
4. 70 − 10 = 60
5. 16
6. 21
7. 18
8. 37
9. 60
10. 9
11. 44
12. 23
13. 52
14. 10
15. 28
16. 5
17. $38
18. 36¢ more
19. Answers will vary.

Page 31
1. 30
2. 40
3. 10
4. 30
5. 0
6. 30
7. 67; 67 + 23 = 90
8. 32; 32 + 18 = 50
9. 34; 34 + 46 = 80
10. 7; 7 + 63 = 70
11. 23; 23 + 17 = 40
12. 33; 33 + 27 = 60
13. 11; 11 + 19 = 30
14. 45; 45 + 45 = 90
15. 93 birds
16. 23 flamingos
17. 5 days

Page 32
1. 71
2. 122
3. 49
4. 65
5. 109
6. 28
7. 102
8. 17
9. 25
10. 152
11. 36
12. 120
13. balloon
14. banner
15. stuffed lion and circus visor
16. circus visor, stuffed lion, banner
17. Answers will vary.

Page 33
1. 2, 7, 2, 4, 9
2. pandas
3. reptiles and giraffes
4. 5 times fewer
5. 9 photographs
6. $0.85; $2.37; $4.15

Mixed Review
1. odd
2. odd
3. odd
4. even
5. 51, 53
6. 55, 50

Page 34
1. 800
2. 1,100
3. 400
4. 1,000
5. 1,100
6. 700
7. 1,700
8. 1,500
9. 900
10. 1,300
11. 600
12. 700
13. 600
14. 900
15. 600
16. 400 people
17. 700 people

Mixed Review
1. 65
2. 46
3. 42

4. 29
5. 105
6. 50
7. 194; 649; 4,122
8. 540, 450, 405
9. 693, 467

Page 35
1. 677
2. 1,378
3. 724
4. 162
5. 407
6. 1,179
7. 894
8. 893
9. 1,099
10. 568
11. 277
12. 847
13. 492
14. 939
15. 839
16. 1, 3, 4, 7, 8, 11, 13
17. 5, 15
18. 2, 6, 9
19. 10, 12, 14
20. 492
21. 716

Page 36
1. 1,125
2. 1,567
3. 1,500
4. 1,431
5. 1,689
6. 963
7. 1,127
8. 893
9. 865
10. 947
11. 918
12. 947
13. 1,109
14. 1,233
15. 719
16. 1,212 rolls and bagels
17. 833 boxes
18. yes
19. 1,320 yards

Page 37
1. $6.89
2. $8.13
3. $11.04
4. $9.87
5. $10.43
6. $13.20

7. $12.29
8. $16.28
9. $17.80
10. $13.72
11. $14.59
12. $12.37
13. $7.81
14. $9.68
15. $4.40
16. less than
17. $5.49
18. $5.55
19. $6.50
20. $5.45

Page 38
1. 200
2. 400
3. 500
4. 700
5. 200
6. 400
7. 800
8. 700
9. 600
10. 300
11. 400
12. 500
13. 200
14. 300
15. 500
16. 300 mi
17. about 700 mi
18. Answers will vary.

Page 39
1. 217; 217 + 644 = 861
2. 426; 426 + 427 = 853
3. 544; 544 + 46 = 590
4. 603; 603 + 145 = 748
5. 327
6. 718
7. 602
8. 925
9. 537
10. 250
11. 355
12. 225
13. 528
14. 503
15. 132 mi
16. 962 people
17. 555
18. 490
19. 461

20. 604
21. 531
Ring 17. and 20.

Page 40
1. subtract; 303 pages
2. add; 856 inns and motels
3. $0.74 less
4. Molly is 14 years old. Brenda is 2 years old.
5. Mr. Carr is 42; Mrs. Carr is 36.
6. his reading homework
7. Answers will vary. Sample answers: 456 – 345; 842 – 731; 654 – 543; The top digit is 1 greater than the bottom digit in each place.

Page 41
1. 87
2. 581
3. 377
4. 537
5. 114
6. 190
7. 135
8. 265
9. 20
10. 344
11. 151
12. 97
13. 33 mi more
14. 495 mi
15. Answers will vary.

Page 42
1. b
2. b
3. c
4. a
5. c

Mixed Review
1. 7,000
2. 700,000
3. 700
4. 70,000

Page 43
1. 96
2. 524
3. 512
4. 322
5. 12
6. 154
7. 108
8. 535
9. 418
10. 199
11. 500
12. 400
13. 200
14. 200
15. 104 more kilometers per hour
16. 311 more kilometers
17. 414; Children should show 7 flats and 3 units; then regroup 1 flat as 10 longs and 1 long as 10 units; and then cross out 2 flats, 8 longs, and 9 units.

Page 44
1. 1,178
2. 696
3. 7,001
4. 646
5. 5,604
6. 8,316
7. 4,007
8. $2.05
9. $0.10
10. $10.20
11. $0.80
12. Answers will vary.

Page 45
1. 4 + 8 + 7 = 19; 19 mi
2. 16 – 9 = 7; 7 mi
3. Jo, 11 mi; Caroline, 14 mi
4. Violet, Arthur, Mel, Chip
5. less than; $0.24
6. $3.18
7. 5 + 5 + 3 = 13; 13 mi

Page 46
1. Monday
2. Thursday
3. April 20
4. April 5
5. 30 days
6. April 14
7. Saturday
8. 9 days
9. April 28
10. Since February is exactly 4 weeks long, March 1 (and all the other dates) fall on the same day in February.

Page 47
1. to watch a movie
2. to read a book
3. to make your bed
4. 6 hours
5. 40 minutes
6. yes
7. no
8. 2 minutes
9. 15 hours
10. The minutes and hours pass quickly when you are enjoying yourself; you are not aware of the time.

Page 48
1. 11:00
2. 3:00
3. 7:00
4. 10 minutes
5. 45 minutes
6. 30 minutes
7. 3:00
8. on the 9

Mixed Review
1. 1,432
2. 526
3. 7,358
4. 1,139
5. 9,884

Page 49
1. 10:15, 1:45, 4:30
2. 11:15, 2:45, 5:30
3. 10:45, 2:15, 5:00
4. 10:30, 2:00, 4:45
5. 3:30
6. 3:15
7. 9:00, nine o'clock
8. 5:15, five-fifteen
9. 7:30, seven-thirty

Page 50
1. 10, 15, 20, 25
2. 10, 15, 20
3. 10, 15, 20, 25, 30
4. 10, 15, 20
5. 4:34
6. 7:39
7. 3:24
8–10. Check work.

Page 51
1. 4:30
2. 6:45
3. Men's basketball
4. 6:30
5. 1 hour
6. 45 minutes
7. 6:50
8. 345 boys and girls
9. Answers will vary.

Page 52
1. 9:15
2. 2:15
3. 11:30
4. 3
5. 2:45
6. Andy, Len, Debra, Matt
7. minutes
8. hours
9. minutes
10. minutes

Page 53
1. 48¢
2. 80¢
3. 48¢
4. 86¢
5–7. Answers will vary. Possible answers are given.
5. three quarters, 1 nickel, 3 pennies
6. 1 quarter, 2 dimes, 2 pennies
7. 2 quarters, 1 dime, 1 nickel
8. 89¢
9. 2 quarters, 2 pennies
10. no, yes, yes, no

Page 54
1. $2.38
2. $6.12
3. $3.95
4. $1.17
5. $2.46
6. $5.88
7. no
8. 2 pennies
9. 5 $1 bills, 3 quarters, 1 dime, 1 penny

Page 55
1. a
2. c
3. $0.29
4. yes
5. yes
6. $9.53

Mixed Review
1. $7.74
2. $11.22
3. $5.51
4. $12.13
5. $1.64

Page 56
1–3. Answers may vary.
1. 3 pennies, 1 nickel, 2 quarters
2. 2 pennies, 2 dimes
3. 3 pennies, 2 quarters, 2 $1 bills
4. 2 pennies, 1 nickel, 1 dime, 1 quarter
5. 2 pennies, 1 quarter
6. 1 penny, 1 nickel, 1 half dollar
7. $2.21
8. next week
9. 3 dimes, 1 penny
10. 4 dimes or 1 quarter, 3 nickels
11. 1 quarter, 1 dime, 1 nickel, 1 penny
12. 4 quarters

Page 57

1. Answers will vary.
   Possible answer:
   5 quarters,
   4 pennies
2. Answers will vary.
   Possible answers:
   1 $5 bill,
   3 quarters,
   2 dimes; 5 $1 bills,
   9 dimes, 1 nickel
3. $13.92
4. $3.16
5. 10 dimes
6. Answers will vary.
   Possible answer:
   6 quarters, 3 dimes
7. $1.35; $1.40;
   $1.50; $1.75; $2.00

Page 58

1. 6, 6
2. 15, 15
3. 14, 14
4. 6, 6
5. 6 cards
6. 12 stickers
7–9. Check pictures.
7. 12, 12
8. 18, 18
9. 21, 21
10. 4 + 4 = 8;
    2 fours = 8

Page 59

1. 8 + 8 = 16;
   2 x 8 = 16
2. 6 + 6 + 6 = 18;
   3 x 6 = 18
3–5. Check drawings.
6. 15 airplanes
7. 4 + 4 + 4 + 4 = 16;
   4 x 4 = 16; 16 mini-
   cars
8. 5 + 5 + 5 = 15;
   3 x 5 = 15
9. 5 + 5 + 5 + 5 + 5 =
   25; 5 x 5 = 25

Page 60

1. 2 + 2 + 2 + 2 = 8;
   2 x 4 = 8
2. 3 + 3 + 3 + 3 = 12;
   4 x 3 = 12
3. 4 + 4 + 4 = 12;
   3 x 4 = 12
4. 18 dolls
5. 20 rare pennies
6. 8 x 2 = 16

Page 61

1. 10
2. 12
3. 16
4. 4 x 2 = 8
5. 2 x 7 = 14
6. 2 x 3 = 6
7. 10
8. 18
9. 8
10. 14
11. 16
12. 12
13. 6 x 2 = 12; 12
    roses
14. 24 + 36 + 48 =
    108;
    108 flowers
15. Marco 10;
    Juana 20;
    Luci 17

Page 62

1. 58, 63, 68
2. baby, baby, mama
3. 15 outfits
4. Check sequence.
5. Wednesday
6. $1.25; yes

Mixed Review
1. 600
2. 100
3. 800
4. 100
5. 1,700
6. 12:45
7. 9:17

Page 63

1. 24
2. 12
3. 18
4. 4 x 3 = 12
5. 3 x 7 = 21
6. 3 x 9 = 27
7. 6
8. 27
9. 24
10. 21
11. 15
12. 18
13. 15 footballs
14. 41 golf balls
15. Check drawings.
    Edward; José: 30
    photos; Edward: 36
    photos

Page 64

1–3. Check drawings.
1. 32
2. 8
3. 28
4. 24
5. 27
6. 8
7. 28
8. 36
9. 21
10. 9
11. 24
12. 16
13. 20
14. 24 buttons
15. 25 buttons
16. 8
17. 12
18. 16

Page 65

1–3. Check drawings.
1. 20
2. 15
3. 30
4. 40
5. 10
6. 35
7. 25
8. 45
9. 28
10. 5
11. 24
12. 36
13. 20
14. +
15. x
16. –
17. 5 x 5 = 25;
    25 cents
18. 40 cents change;
    60 cents purchase
19. 6
20. 5 and 5

Page 66

1. 0
2. 8
3. 0
4. 7
5. 0
6. 3
7. 9
8. 0
9. 0
10. 10
11. 0
12. 6
13. 0

14. 3
15. 0
16. 0
17. 1
18. 0
19. 5
20. 0
21. 4
22. 0
23. 0
24. 2
25. 8 stickers
26. 24 more scented
    stickers

Mixed Review
1. 423,016
2. 97,130
3. 840,631
4. 202,020

Page 67

1. 7 x 3 = 21 squares
2. 4 x 4 = 16 squares;
   Drawings should
   be a large square
   that is 4 units wide
   and 4 units long.
3. 4 x 8 = 32 panes
4. 20 stickers
5. 1:45
6. Check problems.

Page 68

1. 12
2. 21
3. 10
4. 14
5. 24
6. 18
7. 32
8. 25
9. 9
10. 12
11. 16
12. 18
13. 12
14. 27
15. 20
16. 15
17. 30
18. 10
19. 12
20. 45
21. 6 red rings
22. 20 mats
23. 45¢
24. 63 shells
25. 3 x 4 = 12
26. 2 x 6 = 12

Page 69
1. 3 x 3 = 9
2. 2 x 5 = 10
3. 4 x 5 = 20
4. 2 x 8 = 16
5. 3 x 6 = 18
6. 4 x 4 = 16
7. 3 x 3 = 9;
   4 x 4 = 16
8. 49, yes
9. 24, no
10. 36, yes
11. 30, no
12. 56, no
13. 64, yes

Mixed Review
1. 593
2. 196
3. 245
4. 11,371
5. $4.11
6. 8; 4 x 2 = 8
7. 25; 5 x 5 = 25

Page 70
1–4. Check number
   lines.
1. 54
2. 48
3. 30
4. 42
5. 18
6. 24
7. 36
8. 48
9. 30
10. 64
11. 32
12. 30
13. 45
14. 35
15. 42
16. 54
17. 48 tapes
18. $16.98
19. 7
20. 6

Page 71
1. 63
2. 21
3. 14
4. 56
5. 42
6. 63
7. 35
8. 28
9. 56

10. 21
11. 63
12. 27
13. 16
14. 24
15. 36
16. 35
17. 18
18. 48
19. 49
20. 56
21. $9.68
22. 56 boats
23. about 28 days
24. about 364 days

Page 72
1. 0, 8, 16, 24, 32,
   40, 48, 65, 64, 72
2. 56
3. 36
4. 64
5. 40
6. 63
7. 16
8. 24
9. 72
10. 32
11. 48
12. 24 toy rings
13. $2.77
14. 40
15. 64
16. 80
17. 200

Page 73
1. b
2. a; $5.59
3. a; 63¢
4. b
5. more
6. small
7. Answers will vary.

Page 74
1. 27
2. 36
3. 9
4. 18
5. 63
6. 81
7. 45
8. 72
9. 72
10. 63
11. 36
12. 54

13. 0
14. 45
15. 28
16. 36
17. 48
18. 36
19. 18
20. 27
21. 9 years old
22. 63 years old
23. 1, 9, 9
24. 2, 18, 18
25. 3, 27, 27
26. 4, 36, 36

Page 75
1. 18
2. 24
3. 12
4. 40
5. 27
6. 54
7. 45
8. 64
9. 72
10. 24
11. 63
12. 54
13. 56
14. 30
15. 81
16. 64
17. 49
18. 42
19. 24 teddy bears
20. 5:50
21. 3
22. 5
23. 7
24. 8
25. 6
26. 4
27. 5
28. 4

Page 76
1. 15
2. 35
3. 72
4. 14
5. 8
6. 36
7. 24
8. 42
9. 16
10. 54
11. 40
12. 7

13. 45
14. 0
15. 35
16. 72
17. 36
18. 21
19. 4
20. 0
21. 9
22. 8
23. 0
24. 7
25. 6
26. 9
27. $69.90
28. $24

Mixed Review
1. 90,000; 900,000;
   900
2. 2 pennies, 1 nickel,
   1 dime, 4 $1 bills

Page 77
1. Answers will vary.
   Possible answers:
   puffy paint and any
   marker; glitter paint
   and thin or medium
   marker.
2. Answers will vary.
   Possible answers:
   a vest or sweatshirt
   and any one paint
   and marker; a
   jacket, thin marker,
   and puffy paint.
3. $17.17
4. 21 paints
5. Answers will vary.

Page 78
1. 6, 2, 3, 3
2. 21, 3, 7, 7
3. 12, 3, 4, 4
4. 3
5. 2
6. 5
7. 7
8. 4, 2
9. 9, 3
10. 16, 4

Core Skills: Math, Grade 3, Answer Key (cont.)

Page 79
1. 4, 4
2. 3, 3
3. 3, 3
4–6. Check drawings.
4. 5
5. 2
6. 6
7. Drawings should show 4 groups of 2.
8. 5 erasers
9. Answers will vary. Possible answer: Give my friend 18 counters and ask her to separate the counters into 3 groups with the same number of counters in each group. Then, ask how many groups there are and how many counters are in each group. Then, write the division sentence $18 \div 3 = 6$.

Page 80
1. 21, 3
2. 20, 5
3. $4 \times 6 = 24$; $6 \times 4 = 24$; $24 \div 6 = 4$; $24 \div 4 = 6$
4. $5 \times 2 = 10$; $2 \times 5 = 10$; $10 \div 5 = 2$; $10 \div 2 = 5$
5. $3 \times 9 = 27$; $9 \times 3 = 27$; $27 \div 3 = 9$; $27 \div 9 = 3$
6. Drawings should show 6 groups of 3.
7. 24 crayons
8. 2
9. 3
10. 6
11. 5

Page 81
1. 6
2. 5
3. 3
4. 5
5. 6
6. 2
7. 4
8. 2
9. 6
10. 8
11. 9
12. 5
13. 3
14. 7
15. $6
16. 6

Mixed Review
1. 24
2. 63
3. 24
4. 45
5. 56
6. 24
7. $7.95
8. $4.21

Page 82
1. $5 \times 6 = 30$; 30 min
2. $3 \times 5 = 15$; 15 classes
3. $20 \div 5 = 4$; 4 pieces
4. $12 \div 4 = 3$; 3 roses
5. 28 days
6. $24
7. 3 duets
8. 5 duets
9. 7 duets
10. 9 duets

Page 83
1. $12 \div 4 = 3$ or $12 \div 3 = 4$
2. $18 \div 3 = 6$ or $18 \div 6 = 3$
3. 4
4. 6
5. 7
6. 4
7. 9
8. 8
9. 3
10. 2
11. ÷
12. ×
13. ÷
14. ×
15. 2:00
16. $2.85
17. 8 corners
18. 18 corners

Page 84
1. 6
2. 5
3. 6
4. 4
5. 7
6. 3
7. 5
8. 9
9. 8
10. 6
11. 8
12. 9
13. 3
14. 2
15. 3
16. 8
17. 6
18. 5
19. 7
20. 5
21. 7
22. 9
23. 8
24. 9
25. 4 students
26. 16 minutes
27. fewer
28. fewer

Page 85
1. 3
2. 4
3. 2
4. 6
5. 5
6. 3
7. 4
8. 5
9. 6
10. 6
11. 7
12. 9
13. 7
14. 6
15. 7
16. 8
17. 5
18. 5
19. 5
20. 8
21. 6
22. 6
23. 9
24. 1
25. 4
26. 4
27. 40 strands
28. 5 necklaces
29. 2 quarters
30. 5 quarters
31. 15 nickels
32. 40 nickels

Page 86
1. 1
2. 0
3. 7
4. 5
5. 8
6. 0
7. 1
8. 0
9. 0
10. 4
11. 5
12. 1
13. 6
14. 1
15. 9
16. 1
17. $60 - 25 = 35$; 35 min
18. $8 \times 4 = 32$; 32 jars
19. $87 + 18 = 105$; 105 pieces
20. $36 \div 9 = 4$; 4 pounds
21. 4
22. 3
23. 5
24. 4
25. 4
26. 3

Page 87
1. $0.27
2. 15 cars
3. $28.94
4. 80 models
5. 11 cars
6. $2.73

Mixed Review
1. Ring 597, 613, 624, 555, 580, and 648.
2. 616
3. 1,100
4. 87
5. $10.56
6. $3.21

Core Skills: Math, Grade 3, Answer Key (cont.)

Page 88
1–3. Check drawings.
1. 4; 4 rows of 4
2. 2; 5 rows of 2
3. 1; 5 rows of 1
4. 6
5. 6
6. 5
7. 7
8. 3
9. 7
10. 3
11. 5
12. 6
13. 7
14. 4
15. 8
16. 8
17. 8
18. 4
19. 1
20. 3
21. 9
22. 4
23. 9
24. 2:47
25. 4 workers
26. 15 ÷ 3 = 5;
    15 ÷ 5 = 3
27. 12 ÷ 2 = 6;
    12 ÷ 6 = 2
28. 4 ÷ 1 = 4;
    4 ÷ 4 = 1

Page 89
1. 4
2. 4
3. 5
4. 3
5. 4
6. 6
7. 4
8. 6
9. 5
10. 3
11. 3
12. 4
13. 4
14. 3
15. 6
16. 6
17. 3
18. 5
19. 4
20. 802, 840, 885
21. 32 cartons
Mixed Review
1. 14,379

2. 302,860
3. 4 x 3 = 12;
    3 x 4 = 12;
    12 ÷ 4 = 3;
    12 ÷ 3 = 4

Page 90
1. 3
2. 9
3. 0
4. 2
5. 4
6. 6
7. 9
8. 7
9. 8
10. 0
11. 5
12. 7
13. 4
14. 1
15. 3
16. 5
17. 9
18. 0
19. 2
20. 8
21. 9
22. 8
23. 6
24. 6
25. 6
26. 7
27. 8
28. 8
29. 7
30. 7
31. quotient: 6;
    divisor: 3
32. 4 kittens
33. a; $0.12

Page 91
1. 28 patients
2. 3 doctors
3. 18 nurses
4. 46 inches tall
5. Jo, Meg, Bee, Juan
6. 4 parents' books

Page 92
1. 2
2. 4
3. 1
4. 7
5. 6
6. 3
7. 9
8. 8

9. 5
10. 2
11. 7
12. 4
13. 9
14. 8
15. 3
16. 6
17. 0
18. 4
19. 9
20. 1
21. x
22. ÷
23. ÷
24. ÷
25. 1,499 plants
26. 7 mums
27. 4 hr
28. 7 hr

Page 93
1. 8
2. 0
3. 7
4. 6
5. 7
6. 3
7. 5
8. 9
9. 2
10. 0
11. 3
12. 4
13. 8
14. 6
15. 7
16. 1
17. 9
18. 6
19. 8
20. 9
21. 9
22. 8
23. 9 problems
24. more subtraction
    problems
Mixed Review
1. 11,701
2. 7,430
3. 412
4. $109.30
5. $2.44

Page 94
1. 6
2. 4
3. 9
4. 9

5. 2
6. 9
7. 8
8. 3
9. 4
10. 6
11. 9
12. 9
13. 1
14. 8
15. 6
16. 5
17. 0
18. 7
19. 9
20. 3
21. 9 students
22. $45
23. 6 and 8
24. Jon: 2 runs;
    Kristi: 6 runs
25. Check problems.

Page 95
1–3. Check drawings.
    Possible answers
    given.
1. 3 rows of 5;
    1 row of 2
2. 4 rows of 2;
    1 row of 1
3. 5 rows of 4;
    1 row of 3
4. 4)15
5. 6)37
6. 7)18
7. 7 r1
8. 5 r1
9. 2 r2
10. 9 r2
11. 1 r4
12. 8 r1
13. 2 r3
14. 3 r2
15. 5 r4
16. 8 r1
17. 3 r3
18. 2 r2
19. 1 r4
20. 5 r4
21. 4 r1
22. 8 cards each,
    1 left over
23. 4 cards each,
    1 left over
24. 6 cards each,
    1 left over

Page 96
1–4. Methods will vary. Possible answers are given.
1. a, b, c, or d; about 24 calls
2. b or c; 48,876 students
3. a, b, or d; 11:45
4. a or b; Sue, Stan, Jeff
5. 12:45
6. 169 pages
7. 28, 35, 42
8. 36, 30, 24
9. 28, 36, 44
10. 35, 45, 55

Page 97
1. cylinder
2. sphere
3. rectangular prism
4. pyramid
5. cube
6. cone
7. pyramid
8. rectangular prism
9. Answers will vary.

Page 98
1. circle
2. rectangle
3. triangle
4. pentagon
5. circle
6. square
7. square
8. rectangle
9. triangle
10. circle
11. pentagon
12–14. Answers will vary.

Page 99
1. 3 line segments
2. 5 line segments
3. 4 line segments
4. right angle
5. less than
6. greater than
7–8. Check drawings.
9. STOP
10. YIELD
11. street name

Page 100
1. yes
2. no
3. yes
4. Ring middle figure.
5. Ring last figure.
6. Ring last figure.
7. Answers will vary but should include the fact that the figures are the same size and shape.

Mixed Review
1. 15
2. 32
3. 4
4. 9
5. 4 r1
6. 4 r2
7. 2 r2
8. 7 r1
9. 1 r3

Page 101
1. yes
2. yes
3. no
4. yes
5. yes
6. no
7–9. Answers will vary. Check answers.
10–11. Check drawings.

Page 102
1. Friday: 17 min; Saturday: 20 min
2. fifth day: 16 pennies; sixth day: 32 pennies
3. 4:23
4. 14; 18
5. Check drawings.

Page 103
1–7. Answers will vary.
8. Answers will vary. Possible answers: James can measure each side and then add the lengths; he can count the units as he moves around the window.

Page 104
1–3 Answers will vary. Check shapes.
4. 8 sq units
5. 12 sq units
6. 6 sq units
7. 16 sq units
8. 15 sq units
9. 18 sq units
10. 8 sq units
11. 12 sq units
12. 24 sq units
13. Answers may vary. Possible answers: I counted the units; I found the number of groups of 4 square units and multiplied that number by 4.

Page 105
1. 8 cubes
2. 12 cubes
3. 11 cubes
4. 10 cubes
5. 24 cubes
6. 18 cubes
7. 11 cubes
8. 3 cubes
9. 19 cubes

Mixed Review
1. 855
2. 392
3. 6,972
4. $1.11
5. $21.25
6. x
7. ÷
8. ÷
9. x

Page 106
1. (3, 1)
2. (4, 3)
3. (6, 4)
4. (2, 5)
5. (5, 6)
6. (1, 5)
7. (4, 6)
8. (8, 5)
9. E
10. C
11. J
12. D
13. BE
14. 18 eggs
15. $0.83
16. 8 cakes
17. (4, 3)
18. (1, 4)
19. (5, 1)
20. (2, 4)

Page 107
1. Wednesday
2. 10 more tickets
3. Check tables.
4. Titles will vary.
5. 4
6. 338 hot lunches
7. 5 students; all the numbers have 5 as a factor.

Page 108
1. 1 in.
2. 3 in.
3. 6 in.
4–6. Check lines.
7. Accept reasonable answers.
8. 3 in.
9. 10 in.
10. 10 in. wide

Page 109
1. 11 inches
2. 100 yards
3. 20 yards
4. 2 miles
5. 2 feet
6. 20 miles
7. Check drawings. 36 in.
8. 16 ft
9. 32 days

Page 110
1. 1 quart
2. 1 gallon
3. 5 gallons
4. 1 quart
5. c
6. gal
7. gal
8. pt
9. 4, 10, 3, 4, 6
10. 2 quarts
11. 8 cups
12. 4 pints
13. 2 quarts
14. 5 pt

Page 111
1. ounce
2. pound
3. ounce
4. pound
5. 1 pound
6. 8 ounces
7. 25 pounds
8. 10 ounces
9. less than
10. 24 ounces or
    1 pound 8 ounces

Mixed Review
1. 36
2. 9
3. 56
4. 2
5. 9
6. 8
7. 8
8. 8
9. 2
10. 1

Page 112
1. 120°F
2. 30°F
3. 85°F
4. 68°F
5. 46°F
6. 80°F
7. 22°F
8. 62°F
9. no
10. snow suit
11. jacket and pants
12. shirt and shorts
13. swimsuit

Page 113
1. 7 lanes
2. 16 in.
3. 6 people
4. $48.20
5. Max is seventh
   in line.

Page 114
1. 8 cm
2. 5 cm
3–5. Check lines.
6. 52 cm
7. 9 cm
8–10. Answers will
   vary.

Page 115
1. 8 meters
2. 1 meter
3. less
4. more
5. more
6. less
7. m
8. km
9. cm
10. about 56 min
11. 65 m
12. Ring 1,000-meter
    run; 1,500-meter
    run; 10,000-meter
    run

Page 116
1. milliliter
2. milliliter
3. liter
4. 2 L
5. 250 mL
6. 6 L
7. 325 mL
8. 350 mL
9. more
10. 5 L
11. Answers will vary.

Page 117
1. gram
2. gram
3. kilogram
4. kilograms
5. grams
6. Vic
7. Diego, Mac
8. Cory: 25 kg;
   Jake: 26 kg

Mixed Review
1. $6.04
2. $29.72
3. 364
4. 6,465
5. 7,102
6. Ring second and
   fourth shapes.

Page 118
1. 90°C
2. 0°C
3. 20°C
4. 20°C
5. 30°C
6. −5°C
7. 12°C
8. 26°C
9. −10°C

10. 135°C
11. 130°C
12. Newton, 11°C;
    Las Palos, 21°C;
    Richmond, 26°C;
    Shannon, 31°C

Page 119
1. broad jump
2. 6 students
3. $1.53
4. 20 in.
5. 24 yd
6. 45 min
7. Pool B; 4 m farther

Page 120
1. $\frac{4}{5}$; four fifths
2. $\frac{2}{4}$; two fourths
3. $\frac{1}{3}$; one third
4. $\frac{3}{4}$; three fourths
5. $\frac{5}{8}$; five eighths
6. $\frac{2}{6}$
7. $\frac{4}{5}$
8. $\frac{4}{4}$
9. $\frac{1}{3}$
10. $\frac{2}{5}$
11. $\frac{4}{6}$
12–14. Shade one
fourth.

Page 121
1. $\frac{5}{6}$; part of a whole
2. $\frac{4}{7}$; part of a group
3. $\frac{3}{4}$; part of a whole
4. $\frac{3}{8}$; part of a group
5. $\frac{2}{5}$; part of a group
6. $\frac{1}{4}$; part of a whole
7. $\frac{3}{8}$
8. $\frac{2}{5}$
9–10. Check drawings.

Page 122
1. $\frac{1}{3}$ of 6 = 2
2. $\frac{1}{3}$ of 12 = 4
3. $\frac{1}{3}$ of 9 = 3
4. $\frac{1}{5}$ of 5 = 1
5. $\frac{1}{5}$ of 10 = 2
6. $\frac{1}{5}$ of 15 = 3
7. 3 apples

8. $2
9. 12 circles,
   4 circles,
   8 circles

Page 123
1. true
2. false
3. true
4. false
5. true
6. false
7. 4
8. 1
9. 4
10. 2
11. 1
12. 3

Mixed Review
1. 15
2. 40
3. 49
4. 36
5. 54
6. 0
7. 8
8. 9
9. 7
10. 6
11. 6

Page 124
1. <
2. >
3. >
4. <
5. =
6. >
7. =
8. >
9. <
10. Greta
11. more milk
12. The pizza that is
    cut into 6 parts has
    larger pieces.
    When there are
    more parts, the
    pieces are smaller.

Page 125
1–2. Check drawings.
3. b
4. b
5. $1\frac{3}{4}$, 2, $2\frac{1}{4}$
6. Yoki
7. 3 pizzas
8. $2\frac{1}{4}$, $2\frac{2}{3}$, $1\frac{3}{4}$;
   $1\frac{3}{4}$, $2\frac{1}{4}$, $2\frac{2}{3}$